D0908161

The far side of
DESPAIR

The far side of
DESPAIR

Russell K. Hampton

A personal account of depression

Nelson-Hall Chicago

Library of Congress Cataloging in Publication Data

Hampton, Russell K. 1931–

    The far side of despair.

    1. Depression, Mental—Personal narratives.
I. Title. DNLM: 1. Depression—Personal
narratives. WM207H232f
RC537.H32   362.2 B   74–33177
ISBN 0–88229–106–8

Sticks and stones may break my bones; but words can destroy me.

—Anonymous

The grass grows over the graves, time overgrows the pain. The wind blew away the traces of those who had departed; time blows away the bloody pain and the memory of those who did not live to see dear ones again—and will not live, for brief is human life, and not for long is any of us granted to tread the grass.

—Mikhail Sholokhov

Contents

Preface

Berserk Man Kills Wife, Children and Self reads a headline from a recent newspaper. It's not so unusual as it is tragic. Suicide is a leading cause of death in America. Alcoholism is a national social and economic concern. More than half of the hospital beds in our country are filled by mentally disturbed people. The battered child syndrome is familiar to social workers, health agencies, and police departments. Crime, especially of the violent variety, is endemic. The compendium of tragedy wrought by humans on their fellows is almost infinite. It is matched only by examples of man's love and compassion for his fellowman.

What a paradox our lives are! All around us are human tragedies, while at the same time we can see mankind's triumphs. The triumphs, however, will take care of themselves. The tragedies require our attention.

The more dramatic disasters are certainly more compelling. But the little sadnesses, the small afflictions, the minor disappointments are common to us all. In that sense, we have shared our sufferings in common. By the same token, we have all been warmed by a friend's care, a child's joy, a lover's warmth, a stranger's compassion.

I would like to tell you about my experiences with some of the joys and the tragedies when I was twenty-nine years old. I suffered an emotional breakdown. Assailed by anxiety attacks and devastating depressions and paralyzed by despair and panic, I went into a psychiatric ward of a hospital where I spent six months in therapy and in "care." Later, my weekly sessions of individual therapy with a psychiatrist continued for about four years. Following this, I went through two years of group therapy led jointly by a psychiatrist and a pastoral counselor.

My problems were not so dramatic. I didn't shoot anybody or write threatening letters to the FBI. I simply hurt so badly that I felt I could not ever live again. Most people who hurt like I did, and there are many who do and will, suffer in relative silence. Nobody really ever knows how they feel, or why they are frittering their lives away, or alienating their friends, or failing to make a living, or drowning in alcohol or drugs. They plod on through life blindly hoping that tomorrow will be better and brighter. Sadly, those hopes are too often only illusions. My aim is to shed a little light on the dynamics of this despair. Perhaps understanding will engender compassion and from compassion may come caring.

Shortly before I was scheduled to complete my doctorate at a major university in the Southeast, I suffered a breakdown. After six months in a hospital, I was readmitted to the graduate program at the university and a year later received my degree. Following this I spent considerable time in individual and group therapy.

I have agonized over my life and tried to discover what made it come apart and how I managed to get it back together again.

At this time I administer a psychological services program

for a large agency. I'm married, have three children, and do limited private practice as a psychologist helping handicapped and disturbed children and their parents. Most of the time I'm pretty happy. I find life to be exciting and boring, happy and sad, bright and dark. In short, it's a conglomeration of "blooming, buzzing confusion." But perhaps that's the way it is for everyone. I hope that this articulation of my feelings and fears, my triumphs and failures, will help somebody else, perhaps you, to deal with life in a more constructive, mature fashion.

UNIVERSITY MEMORIAL HOSPITAL
ADMITTING DEPARTMENT
PSYCHIATRY

Date: *1 / 14 / 61*
Patient's Name: *Hampton, Russell K.*
Age: *29*   **Birthdate:** *8 / 20 /31*
Address: *Apt. 4B, Student Village, University Station*
Occupation: *graduate student, teaching assistant*
Next of Kin: *wife, Hampton, Nancy B.*
Children: *none*
Admitting Diagnosis: *acute depressive reaction;*
tentative, pseudoneurotic schizophrenic reaction
Health Insurance: *none*
Admitted to: *Psychiatric Department*
Admitted by: *Dr. W. B. Long*

Initial Report—Admitting Officer

Date: *1 / 14 /61*

I interviewed Russell Hampton, age 29, white male, university doctoral student and teaching assistant, on this date to determine his need for hospitalization. Mr. Hampton was lucid and in good contact, although he was obviously under a great deal of stress. He complained of panic attacks, periods of deep depression, insomnia, and general anxiety. His affective tone during this time was relatively flat and somewhat inappropriate. However, he was not psychotic, nor did he show evidences of hallucinatory or delusional material.

Mr. Hampton was rather open and uninhibited in discussing his difficulties, and revealed a great deal of his emotional life on the initial interview. I'm not sure whether this is a manifestation of his inability to control his impulses and conscious processes, or if it reflects his training in counseling and psychology. Because he showed such gross evidences of difficulty in so many varied dimensions of his life processes, I am inclined to believe his difficulty may be more than a simple acute depressive process. However, I have given that tentative diagnosis with a view toward changing it to a diagnosis of pseudoneurotic schizophrenic reaction if it is later seen as appropriate.

Mr. Hampton reported that he had had similar feelings of depression at various stages of his life when the demands for independence on him were pressing. He reported such episodes when he went away to college, when he entered the navy, when he married, and when he entered his current doctoral studies. None of these resulted in hospitalization or periods of incapacity.

This young man is anxious for help, insightful, intelligent, and in considerable distress. I believe that he is a good candidate for psychotherapy, and that his acute symptoms should be resolved in a relatively short time. He certainly should be an instructive patient for teaching purposes.

Clinical Observation

Mr. Hampton showed considerable evidence of anxiety and stress including palmar sweating, tremor, and hyperventilation. He was orientated for time and place and showed a clear sensorium. Probing revealed no delusional material or evidence of thought disorder. His mood was appropriate, but showed considerable depression and anxiety. His affect was at an adequate, though somewhat flat, level; and his dependency and ambivalence were high. I do not believe that he is suicidal or homicidal.

I have on this date admitted this man to the Psychiatric Department of University Memorial Hospital for treatment.

W. B. Long, M.D.
Chief Resident Psychiatrist

Of course, this is not the actual admitting information from my case file. That is not available to me. However, I believe that the initial report you have just read is a reasonable approximation of what was said about me at the time I was admitted for psychiatric treatment in my twenty-ninth year.

Down to depression

WHAT I HAVE LIVED is in a large measure what I am. While I don't know your motives for reading this book, I suspect that in one way or another, either you or someone you love has felt the gnawing suspicion of nothingness. This suspicion is the most destructive, debilitating, and frightening emotion in the range of human responses. Difficult to describe, this suspicion suggests that the struggle you make may be worthless, that the game is not worth the candle, that even if you persist and even if you triumph, in the end you will lie down forever having meant little to the world, to the people in it now, or to those to follow. This is the insidious feeling that must be anticipated and guarded against.

The human mind and body can endure anything, provided there is a conviction that the "game" is worthy of the effort. This conviction has enabled man to withstand the worst that fate and other men can conceive—witness the persecution and perseverance of the Jews—the degradation of human dignity occurring so often in the ghettoes of the world. Look at our treatment of our fellows who are sick in spirit and mind. Look at any jail or any mental hospital.

When a man decides that the struggle is not worth the effort, then a kind of death, absolute or relative, can be predicted. How to anticipate this I don't know. Our predictive devices for individuals aren't accurate. Perhaps one could simply ask, "Can you resist pain, unrelenting and unremitting and unlikely to be relieved?" We should not ask the question, however, if we are not prepared to accept responsibility for man's answer.

With me it began as a pain in my chest. It was acute and fairly severe. At least I thought so at the time. I have withstood much worse since, not without considerable whimpering and bitching, I might add. Well, what could it be? Indigestion? I gave voice to this thought, but a sneaky feeling in the back of my mind began to give voice to its thoughts as well: "No, it's not indigestion. It's probably cancer or a heart attack." "No," I argued out loud, "it's indigestion." But "that feeling" didn't hear me. And a slow but growing panic moved over my mind and body.

Almost a month before this, my wife and I had gone to her home to visit an aunt who was dying of cancer. She had not been told, and we were to maintain a cheerful attitude with her. I am sure that she knew, but she was pleasant and optimistic during our visit.

We returned to school and I resumed studying for my doctoral examinations coming up in October. My major fields of study were counseling and school psychology. Like most graduate students I was under considerable pressure. How much of myself I had committed to this milestone in my life I did not then know. Passing the examinations seemed to represent some peak of achievement in my life that even now I am unable to explain. I had to pass! To fail was worse than any alternative. I recognized that I had these feelings, and I also knew that they were exaggerated and unrealistic. Over and over I told myself this. But "I" did not listen. Morbidly, like a person worrying a sore tooth, I would think, "Suppose I fail?" Then a little ripple of dread and horror would pass over me, and with a shudder I would try to think of something else, but with limited success. I feel now that these morbid preoccupations represented, more than anything else, my attempts to prepare myself for failure. But when I tried them out, I found that I would be unable to accept failure, thus the dread and fear.

So the days dragged by. Studying, reading, talking with other students, worrying. Nothing unusual. I was conscious of a considerable amount of anxiety. But "So what," I thought, "everybody else is ready to flip too." Finally the big days came. We took our examinations—a day, and half of another, of written exams. Then came the wait for the verdict.

In about a week, I received a letter from the assistant dean informing me that I had passed the written portion of the tests. I was soon to report to a committee in my department for oral presentations. This was scary, too. I knew the members of my department, and I knew they thought I was a good student. About the only question I can remember being asked during this interview was, "What would be the main focus of emphasis in a program to train counselors if you could make the decisions?" I remember my answer too. I said that I would require trainees to have access to intensive and complete counseling and personal analysis themselves. The point being, of course, that they must know themselves and be at relative peace with what they are before they can give others the help they need. How little I knew of myself.

Panic

Then I experienced my first recognizable period of panic, the first, that is, that I could relate to an outside event. The chairman of my department congratulated me on passing my exams and said that I had made one of the highest recorded marks on the written materials. He went on to say that he and other members of the department had the greatest expectations for my future—that I would undoubtedly make some significant contributions to the field of psychological services in the future. One should be pleased with such praise and encouragement, but I wasn't. I felt intense panic over what it seemed to me that I now had to do. I now had significant eyes on me and had to make some notable contributions!

There may be no rest for the wicked, but compared to the rest that anxious people get, they undoubtedly have a pastoral life. I had successfully entered graduate school, had been awarded a scholarship, passed two years of graduate course work, completed my comprehensive examinations, favorably impressed my major professors and my other instructors, and now I had to make a significant contribution to the field! There was no point at which I could rest. When could I drop my partially pretended and consciously maintained air of studiousness, perseverance, flexibility, and ease of manner? I was in worse shape than I had been in before. I might have been able to recoup somehow if I had failed, but now that I had passed, what?

I must admit, however, that I see many of these things only now. At that time I knew only that I was tired and overwhelmed by feelings that were strange and powerful. Fortunately, at this time I was finishing my formal course work and all that remained was to plan, outline, and complete a dissertation. All that remained—ha! Those of you who have undertaken a doctoral thesis know what a hell of a job that is.

A period of coping

One evening after a leisurely meal and some television watching, I noticed a feeling of discomfort in my lower chest. It felt like a knot. A dose of soda didn't seem to help. By bedtime the knot had grown and with it a considerable pain. It had penetrated to my back in sharp, piercing waves. My mind shifted into high gear, and I began to consider the things that it could be. Indigestion? No, it hurts too much and it hasn't eased yet. Heart attack? No, I said to myself, I'm too young. Nervous spasms? No, I didn't think I felt particularly anxious. Ah, then the joker triumphantly sprang from the deck, a malignancy! It was going to be death for me! My head began to feel as if it had too much blood in it. Anxiety danced madly in my stomach, demanding exit through my mouth. And a crushed feeling, like a childish hurt or resentment, settled on my shoulders. I complained worriedly to my wife, not saying, of course, what I suspected. She tried to reassure me, but I succeeded in worrying her too.

Finally the pain eased and we went to bed. But I didn't sleep for a long time. I went through every imaginable possibility. I pictured myself in a hospital. The doctor told me that I couldn't make it. I had six weeks. (Why do people always have six weeks?) I went through those entire six weeks, on to my final breath, my funeral, and wonder of wonders, on to my wife's subsequent period of mourning, her recovery, new friendships, a courtship, and finally remarriage, and my resulting jealousy. I know this sounds ridiculous, but this is what I was doing. It would be ludicrous were it not for the fact that I was in mortal agony with these thoughts.

My episode of panic over the chest pain gradually subsided over the next few days, and for a week or so things went along about as usual. I would have been willing, I think, to accept a psychosomatic explanation for this if it had occurred prior to taking and passing my comprehensive doctoral exams. But those were behind me now, and it seemed logical to assume that if this was a somatic reaction to stress it would have occurred before, not after, I took my exams. My logic, I have found, is not always in keeping with my emotional reactions!

Things went on as before, But inevitably, another night came with another attack. My panic and unbridled fantasies increased. After this attack, I was frightened enough to go to the infirmary. The doctor there gave me a careful physical examination and took a comprehensive history. He prescribed some drug (a sedative) and suggested a bland diet for a few days. Well, this calmed me down for another week or two. However, soon more pain and a more intense reaction from me. I was in a state of near panic. I was finally and completely convinced that I was dying.

On my next visit, the doctor could see that I was distraught. He made an appointment for a stomach x-ray and for a kidney study. Back in the infirmary a few days later, I felt my level of anxiety somewhat allayed, probably by the attention I was getting.

The stomach x-ray was suggestive of a lesion in the duodenum. In other words, an ulcer. What a relief to learn this! There really was something physically wrong with me. So, when I went on a bland diet with medication and milk, my stomach calmed down a bit. By now my doctor had suggested psychiatric help for me. I was a little stunned at this suggestion. "You mean I've got a neurotic stomach?" I was honestly amazed. This long suffering man had finally reached his limit. "Well, Goddamn," he exclaimed, "you've got an ulcer. What does that tell you?" I was shocked and confused. I told him that I'd see someone in my department for counseling.

I tried. My friend, and major professor, tried. But I was beyond the point of "reconstruction" at the time. The decompensation process was in full momentum. There was the added obstacle of my prior deception in my own department. I had spent so much time and effort on my public personality that I found it impossible to drop it. I gave some flimsy excuse after a couple of sessions and my counselor permitted me to withdraw. I wish now that he had insisted that I stay with him. But if the decision didn't come from me, it probably would have been meaningless. Besides, I am sure insistence would be contrary to his basic beliefs concerning the helping relationship. I wonder how he feels about this now. I was beyond the point of making anything like a mature, capable decision about myself. I didn't know what to do or whom to turn to. My resources and strengths were exhausted and my defenses, so laboriously built, collapsed.

Another day, another doctor

We went to my wife's folks' home for the Christmas holidays. Talking about my newly discovered ulcer and my diet was some relief. And for two or three days, I had some respite. But now the episodes were coming more frequently and were more damaging and frightening. Finally, I woke on the fifth morning of our vacation with a distraught feeling and with profound nausea. My mother-in-law called the doctor. He looked me over, decided it must be the ulcer, and prescribed something for nausea.

I felt a little better, and we went over to my folks' house for a few days. On Christmas day I couldn't get out of the bed. I was so nauseated and so miserable that I could barely talk. Another doctor called. Still more medication. He told me some years later that he thought at the time that I was having a "nervous nausea." But he didn't say anything then. In fact, no one had yet said, "You are having a depressive-emotional attack. There's nothing physically wrong with your stomach."

That afternoon my mother called an internist in the city, an older and wise man. He was cautious and careful and sympathetic and he found out what was wrong with me, but he didn't anticipate its severity. At least he didn't tell me if he did.

That afternoon I was admitted into the hospital in the city for diagnostic study. Dr. W. took a careful history and listened to my long tale of woe. After a thorough physical exam, he ordered an electrocardiogram. When I learned that he had done that, I really was in a tizzy! I tried to appear casual when I asked if he suspected some cardiac trouble. "No," he replied, "but I want to do a thorough check on everything that may possibly be wrong." I was convinced he was lying. He had heard something that sounded bad in my heart! I was convinced of that. I now imagined myself a lifelong invalid or saw myself dropping over dead at any moment.

He left and after awhile a young technician came in wheeling the electrocardiograph machine. She seemed rather uncertain of herself as she attached the leads. I interpreted her behavior as being due to her knowledge that I was very sick. Certainly her rather grim manner did nothing to reassure me. She finally left and I was alone again.

In trying to capture in words my predominant feelings at this time, all I can come up with is "I felt bad." I could hardly talk to anybody. I was sick to my stomach and extremely depressed. I was so tired and lethargic that nothing seemed possible, and worse still, nothing was desirable.

Then Dr. W. came back with a copy of the EKG tape in his hand. "Well," he says, "we're going to have to take another one." "Oh Lord," I groaned to myself, "I must really be in bad shape." But all I said out loud was a calm, "Why?"

"The first test wasn't run properly." He seemed to me to be calculatingly casual, and I didn't believe him for a minute. Later that night I had another period of panic and despair. I cried bitterly late that night, alone in my room, convinced I was dying.

More tests and more probing, including an examination for possible kidney damage. It's amazing what terrible shape you are in when somebody really looks! But all of this testing yielded nothing.

Dr. W. came in my room and sat on the side of the bed. He went over the results of all the lab studies and x-rays. "There's nothing wrong with your heart. The first test was not done properly and the second was perfectly normal. The cystoscopic examination revealed no kidney disorder. And the x-ray showed no ulcer." No ulcer! I was really worried since they had found nothing. "If you've had an ulcer," he continued, "I can see no trace of it now." "Son," he said, "you've just got to change your way of life. You're pushing yourself to the point of exhaustion." I thanked him and soon left the hospital, somewhat relieved.

After a day or so, my wife and I headed back to school. I was so beaten and felt so bad that I had to lie down in the back seat of the car most of the way while she drove. We got back to school and to our apartment. And we went back to our jobs—me to class and work as a teaching assistant; she, back to her work at the university library.

Final decline

Stress, fear, anxiety, and panic are part of everyone's life at some time. These burdens are hard to bear even when one has support and help. Alone, you are crushed, without hope or the promise of relief. Fortunately I did not have to face these trials alone. My wife, in every sense, is a part of me.

I think many times of the anxiety, pain, and heartache that my wife has suffered, with and because of me. I'm sorry that it has been this way for her. But I'm selfishly glad that I had her with me for comforting, for her courage, and for the meaning she has given my life. Without her, I'm convinced, I wouldn't be writing these words now. And her courage has been much greater than that of simply caring for me. And much more demanding because she has insisted that I am and can be somebody, like everybody else. And she has not fallen into the easier snare of taking over for me and letting me drift through life uninvolved. She is involved with me. I like her.

But school and my work were no easier. I submerged myself in studying, trying to force my wildly fluctuating emotions to settle down. I studied and read. I wrote papers and reviewed many more books and journal articles than was necessary for my course work. Sometimes, though, I would read three or four pages and suddenly realize that I didn't have the vaguest notion what I had read. Then I'd go back and read it all over again. Sometimes I would be in such agony that I would almost have to cry aloud in the library. Then I would go outside until I felt I was under control again. I read and worked until I finally was in such misery that I couldn't read at all.

I told two of my professors that I was having panic attacks and depressions. They were all sympathetic and supportive. I talked with the head of my department about my difficulties and asked if this was going to compromise my doctoral work. He was kind and helpful and assured me that it would not. And my subsequent experience with them showed them to be as good as their word. They gave me justice but with a heavy ladling of mercy. But I don't believe now that they realized what a terrible condition I was in.

My illness had begun suddenly and rather severely. For three months I had struggled and had maintained my outward equilibrium, and had stayed on my teaching job and in my doctoral program. But now the disorganization was precipitous. I was rapidly losing my ability and will to recover and reorganize. Panic and depressive attacks were besetting me with increased frequency and with more awesome force. Now I was having four or five attacks a day. Attacks so beyond my control that I literally had to hide when I knew they were coming. If I could get to my apartment, I would sit huddled against the wall in a corner with my knees drawn up to my chest, clinging to them tightly. And my body would shake like that of a malaria victim and I would cry in anguish and pain. Sometimes I would pace the floor, my insides quivering, with every nerve in my body seemingly on the surface of my skin, being scorched by the movement of the air.

When the attacks subsided, I did my job as best I could, went to class, wrote papers, listened to lectures, and took the final exams in the last of the course work I had to take.

Somehow I made A's on all of this work. How I did this, I don't really know. I did manage to pull myself together for extended periods of time. But these periods were becoming shorter and shorter. Finally, the semester was over, and so was I.

I called the school psychiatrist who had seen me two or three times and told him that I was in a panic state, that I could no longer tolerate it. I had to have some help. Something had to be done. He told me to come down to the student infirmary and he would admit me for a few days. I packed my bag, again a little relieved that I was going to get something done for me. I stopped by the library and told my wife where I was going.

I lay in the bed at the infirmary thinking that at last I would get some relief. I was given tranquilizers and, at night, sleeping medication. But it was too little, too late.

I didn't calm down. I was in a state of acute anxiety and agitated depression. The psychiatrist came in twice a day for brief sessions and I think he felt I was calming down a bit. The fact was that I hurt terribly every minute. Occasionally I had a few moments of relative calm and ease. When these moments came, I thought, "Ah, now things will get better. I'll get out of here and finish my degree and maybe even write a book about the horror of mental illness! I'll tell the world about my tragic suffering and show them by my brave and noble works how people with emotional disorders can contribute to society." I know this is asinine, but it's really what I was thinking. I felt ennobled, cleansed through suffering, compassionate, rather more fortunate than those poor clods who led such meaningless lives. My humbling was yet to come. But I didn't know it then.

The psychiatrist let me go home after three or four days. There my newfound sense of noble martyrdom lasted about six hours. I entered the final decline. I soon was so paralyzed with psychic pain that I was almost comatose. I couldn't eat at all and the only sleep I got was in fifteen or twenty minute exhausted periods. I couldn't talk to anyone or even sit up. I couldn't read or watch television, and finally I couldn't hold my head up off my chest. I was in desperate agony.

My mother had stopped by a few days before this. She

said she was on her way to visit some friends. I doubt that now. I am sure she was worried about me and came to see how things were going.

My mother and my wife tried to help: hot soup, back rubs, aspirins, quiet, and dark rooms. What those few days must have done to them!

There was no turning back from my destination. They tried to take me for walks. The psychiatrist must have advised them to keep me busy. Each of them would hold one arm, propping me up. I remember how cold it was. And we walked, and we walked. Finally I couldn't even walk.

In the free moments we talked. We talked about many things. Old wounds and old disappointments; guilts for things done and not done, for things said and not said; for help and sustenance given or withheld. The anguish of my wife was for someone she loved and could not help. That of my mother, for someone she loved and could not help and who was suffering, she was convinced, largely because of her. I guess every mother believes in her heart of hearts that she is responsible for what she has nurtured. In that sense, mothers are doomed (privileged?) to live the lives of their children and to suffer their anguish and savor their triumphs. So we wallowed in anguish, in fear, in guilt, and in self-reproach. Until we finally had to stop.

We all knew that I had to have care, probably in a hospital. My wife and mother left me in the care of a friend, and I was now so distraught that it's probably a good thing that they did. They went to see the college psychiatrist who had been treating me. He agreed that his "first aid" had failed, and they arranged to have me admitted to the psychiatric ward of the student health center and hospital on the campus.

We made our way fearfully up those steps and to the

waiting room. And we sat on a sofa, huddled together, trying to talk about things as if our lives weren't caving in around us.

Soon, I was admitted. Before I walked down the hall, my wife and my mother kissed me and uttered sounds of comfort and hope. As I walked away, I knew that something in my life had ended, an era was over and a time of transition had come.

It was to be nearly six months before I was to walk back down that corridor to leave the hospital. And I was to come to know that hell has no fear for him who has been there. And I would have been there before I came back to the world.

The hospital

2

ENTERING A COMPOUND for mental patients is a most frightening experience. It doesn't matter whether it's a private hospital, a public one, or a ward of a general hospital. The implication is inescapable: "I am unable to care for myself. Without help I can not survive." Precisely the status of an infant. For some persons this may not constitute a particular insult to the self; for me it was unforgettable and almost intolerable.

Still, it had come to that. Bewildered and numb, I had finally reached the point where I was incapable of hiding the intense pain I was feeling. Panic would overtake me along with the all-pervasive depression, and I could only sit in agony and cry. I couldn't sleep or eat, nor did I feel that I could long stand the agonizing anguish of my uncontrollable feelings. I have been told that mental suffering is the most exquisite of all pain. This seems a peculiar way to describe it, but it's accurate. The exacting and precise horror of the emotional devils of anxiety and depression leaves no doubt in the experiencer as to their power and completeness.

I was helpless. A deeper wound to the self-integrity I

cannot imagine. Preservation of the physical self has been called the basic instinct. It isn't. Around us every day are examples of the sacrifice of the physical self in deference to the preservation of other aspects of the self—emotional, moral, and social. Men die in battle rather than bear the title "coward." Buddhist monks give their physical bodies in fiery death to preserve their moral integrity. And emotionally sick people every day surrender what to them is the dubious honor of physical life to preserve psychological wholeness. Then this was the horror to me, the surrender of the things that I had spent twenty-nine years trying to secure—independence, personal and psychological integrity. I had lost it all. My loss was so great that I was almost at the point of requiring care of my physical bodily functions. Fortunately, I was spared that. Psychiatrists call it regression. I call it the epitome of psychological insult.

I'll never forget the words of the admitting officer of the psychiatric ward of the hospital. He probably won't remember now, but his words were like saccharin—sweet at first, but turning exceedingly bitter. He promised relief; at least that's what I heard.

After I had spent some time describing the events and feelings leading up to that moment (and how tired I was of being compelled to go over and over my life, searching for the moment when it went wrong or for those things I had or hadn't done), he responded, "There is no need for you to suffer like that." He implied help then, didn't he? At least I interpreted it that way. The assurance in his tone suggested that the techniques, skills, and tools required were also known and were available. This proved to be an overgenerous assumption on my part. For some time I was convinced that it was just a cruel hoax.

The psychiatric ward occupied the entire sixth floor of the

hospital. On the floor below us were the general surgical patients. They might as well have been in another world. The only exit from the sixth floor was by an elevator which was watched at all times by a nurse or attendant in the front office. At night the doors leading to the elevator were locked.

A small waiting room faced the elevator. At one side were the doors to the corridor leading to the psychiatric ward. The nurses' station was on the opposite side of the room. Through these doors and down the hall were rooms on each side, looking like the doors to rooms in any hospital or motel anywhere. There were about thirty rooms opening onto this straight corridor. About halfway down there was a larger nurses' station surrounded by windows and an intersecting passageway to the dayroom of the ward. The dayroom, or sitting room, was a large room opening onto an outdoor patio. The patio was enclosed by a chain link fence. There were chairs, sofas, and tables in the dayroom along with a television set, a piano, and a pool table. A small kitchen opened off the dayroom.

Miss Wolfe, a nurse, took me to my room. She was starched, crisp, professionally friendly, and briskly competent. She tried to preserve the illusion that this was adult interaction, when both she and I knew that it wasn't. This was an adult dealing with a child, perhaps a well-meaning but slightly incompetent child. This general relationship, based on unsupportable presumptions, adult to adult, was to characterize the total environment of the ward and all the relationships between the "helpers" and the "children." Of course, I am not attempting to report the facts, but only how I felt. At any rate, this orientation became embarrassingly incongruous in times of crisis—when someone cried in the dayroom or became so disturbed that restraint was necessary to prevent injury or when self-feeding was not possible. One needed permission to take an aspirin (an event of such importance and so filled with bureaucratic red tape that you usually just endured the headache). The whole atmosphere of the place was a ridiculous caricature of Victorian family life. The "children" were handled firmly but kindly (eat your dinner and no dawdling). The "mamas" were understanding, but controlling; and the "real life" of the home revolved around the usually absent "papa," the psychiatrist. His word was law and his wishes were to be obeyed by the "children" and the "mamas." He was never wrong, and he was approachable only at prescribed times and places. He could administer punishment (restriction), and he decided what was best for the "children."

I'm sure I've made my point. Upon reflection I feel that the likely reason for the behavior of most of the professional staff in this kind of setting, which is essentially a kind of noninvolvement, is their feelings of frustration and anger at how limited their aid is, and their keen appreciation of the suffering they have accepted the responsibility for relieving, which is beyond their capacity and skills to handle effectively. I believe that when drug treatment reaches the point of relative efficiency in relieving the pain of mental disorder, psychiatrists and others in the mental health professions will expose themselves to those they are trying to help, and they will become involved. At least those who can risk this kind of involvement with others will. Some of them can't.

The self-consciousness of much of this structured institutional behavior (called milieu therapy in the professional journals) was sometimes so embarrassingly contrived that it demanded the skill and versatility of veteran actors on the parts of both the staff and patients to maintain the fiction of a pseudosocial grouping.

The best isn't good

I was in a reputedly excellent psychiatric ward. Known throughout the South, it draws a number of minor celebrities and public figures for treatment of their emotional disorders or drug and alcohol addictions. I was in one of the best treatment facilities available in my section of the country. In fact, it was the best, and it was demoralizing, humiliating, and dehumanizing! God knows what the poorer facilities and the state hospitals do to people if this was the best medical science had to offer.

The ward is operated for the benefit and convenience of the staff, not the patients. Decisions are made that affect the welfare of all, but consultation with patients prior to action is seldom, if ever, offered. In such an atmosphere you are not regarded as a responsible participant in your own growth. You are told, in many subtle ways, many times every day that you are incompetent—"that's why you are here." If you maintain your independence of spirit and belief, you are held to be uncooperative and possibly untreatable. You are a broken object to be fixed. There is no conception or consideration of your stake in the action and interaction with those around you.

You are reminded every day in many ways that you are sick and not to be trusted. Yet, you are held accountable, but not responsible, for your ability to get well.

There are three distinct classes of citizens in the psychiatric ward. At the bottom rung of this ladder are the grossly psychotic and senile people. They are subtly ignored unless they make too much noise or unless they are wealthy or famous. Little effort is expended on understanding their expressions of misery and distress. They are socked with massive drug doses or electricity. And they'd better pull out fast, or they've had it.

The second rung of the ladder is occupied by the neurotic patients, and, to some degree, by attendants. When you contrast the capability and social competency of any given neurotic patient with either the attendant population or the professional staff, you are hard pushed to say who is sick and who isn't. It may be that the major difference between the neurotic patient and the staff is the possession of a good health insurance plan!

I know I listened to some hair-raising recitations of personal difficulties, personality problems, and social dissonance from several members of the staff, both attendants and professionals. Bert, for instance, was one of the favorite attendants. He had a pencil thin mustache, slicked down black hair, and looked as if he had just put down his cue stick in the pool hall. Bert gambled heavily. One week he took several of us for a ride in his new convertible. A few days later he was trying to borrow money for his rent. He told me once that he was so nervous that he had to either take some pills or drink a little if he was going to keep going. He took a job in a mental ward because he thought he would be able to get all the drugs he wanted legitimately from the staff physicians. By the time he found out he couldn't, he liked his job too well to quit. Curiously enough, he was one of the favorite people in the ward. He was compassionate in a way that made it possible to feel that he knew what kind of problems you had. He'd listen attentively, and he'd respond freely, sharing his own experiences with you. He didn't hide his frailties, and certainly didn't try to magnify his power. He was a good psychotherapist. But, of course, he had no more status than the neurotic patients, and no formal influence on what happened on the ward.

Neurotic patients were valued on the ward in a rather peculiar way. They were necessary to the operation of the unit, yet like obstreperous children in a family, they were better out of sight and out of mind. The craziness that was in us was seen as reprehensible, if not downright sinful. Repression of feelings was the order of the day. Expressions of the feelings and experiences that brought us there were not approved! If you persisted in showing openly what was bothering you, you were regarded as uncooperative or even "unsuitable for treatment." This designation resulted in an almost automatic prescription "out," or electric shock, or an increased drug regimen. I know this sounds nutty, but it's true! If you were crazy, you were subtly reprimanded and tacitly chastised as if you had committed some crime that was held to be more shameful than criminal.

Of course, the top of the social hill was occupied by the professional staff, the physicians, nurses, social workers, and psychologists, although the psychologists were strictly auxiliary. They crept in with an apologetic hangdog air, gave their tests, and silently slipped away. The real managers of us all were the nurses. The day to day and moment to moment contacts and programs were products of nurse behavior. The psychiatrists flitted through our lives like the Victorian fathers of old. They were seldom physically present and they were always unapproachable, but they made judgments and decisions for all. It came to amuse me to see how they managed to maintain their social, psychological, and professional distance from the patients. They wore white, long coats just like Sigmund must have worn in the hospital in Vienna in the 1880s. I know why auto mechanics and cooks wear protective clothing, but I wonder why a hospital psychiatrist does?

The psychiatrists never sat in the dayroom and chatted with patients and families, nor did they drink coffee or eat a meal with the patients. In short, they carefully prescribed a limited and sterile kind of interaction, and they protected themselves with great skill. Perhaps they wanted to keep from contaminating the transference relationship! I suspect, in their heart of hearts, they were really ashamed and afraid of their inability to meet the demanding needs of their patients. It takes a strong, secure personality to admit your limitations in the presence of demands for help. Many of them just don't have the psychological guts for the job. The distance they maintain serves to protect them; it does little to facilitate the growth of the people they are taking money from to help.

Surviving is the name of the game

Dehumanizing, demeaning, and growth restricting are how I describe the best of the hospitals for the mentally disturbed. And in spite of this, some people recover. Most manage to merely pull themselves together for another try at the world. A few grow enough to master their lives when they leave such a setting. I think an interesting, but of course impossible, experiment would be to put a hundred or so well-adjusted, normal (whatever that is) people in a "good" mental health institution for six months, and see how many of them would be able to make a satisfactory posthospital adjustment. I'll wager that more than a few would be casualties. One of those casualties was Claude.

I had been sharing a room with Claude for about two months. He was a fifty-six-year-old, red-headed Irishman who had been "retired" early by the publishing firm he had served as an executive for thirty years. After a month or so of enforced leisure, he had downed a bottle of sleeping pills chased with a pint of liquor. He woke up three days later, much to his chagrin, to find himself in the psychiatric ward of the city hospital. He tried to get a discharge, but his daughter threatened to have him committed unless he consented to treatment.

After about twelve shock treatments, he was quieter and a little less bitter and belligerent. He probably would continue to live, but he was subdued and lifeless. He told me he was being discharged at the end of the week.

Claude was a treatment casualty. Certainly his immediate depression and resulting intention to kill himself were relieved. But the circumstances that had forced him to this position had not changed nor had his capacity to cope with them been enlarged. He would leave the hospital no better equipped psychologically to deal with his feelings of helplessness, uselessness, and loneliness.

"What are you going to do now, Claude?" I asked. He looked a bit perplexed before replying, "I don't know." Then he forced a smile and said, "I guess I'll go down to Florida and sit in the sun and enjoy life." This was followed by a hollow laugh. He left on a Friday, and I didn't hear from him again.

Shocking

Electric-convulsive therapy (referred to as ECT) is a misunderstood, maligned, and feared treatment, seldom the treatment of choice. Even many psychiatrists who use it frequently and effectively fear and despise its use. They often wait until everything else fails before they try it. Commonly, they try a course of psychotherapy (about which I will say more later) or drugs or Milieu Therapy, which is a fancy name for a hospital regime. If the condition is not improved and if the condition is utterly debilitating to the patient, they will prescribe a course of ECT (especially in depressive illnesses). Then they are busy assuring patient and relatives that it is not to be feared or dreaded.

The facts are that ECT, for some disorders, is amazingly effective for the relief of suffering and the restoration of the patient to some semblance of normal life. Usually, the disorders associated with depression and sometimes acute agitation respond best to shock treatment. Psychiatrists dislike it primarily because they do not know why and how it works. Neither does anyone else, for that matter. There are some fifty theories in the technical literature which try to explain what happens in the treatment. None of them has been satisfactorily verified.

Another probable reason that the treatment is disliked is that it constitutes an assault on the individual. Though designed to produce benefits to the assaulted, it is an assault nevertheless. It is not only a physical assault on the physical being, but an attack on the essence of being, the mind.

ECT consists basically of subjecting the brain to a small electrical charge. This, in reduction to basics, is shock treatment. There are some effects that have nothing to do with the psychological effects of the treatment. The current causes unconsciousness, convulsive spasms, and certain temporary physiological changes. Occasionally a bone is broken, but rarely do serious physical consequences occur. Nowadays the patient is usually asleep from a mild anesthetic after having been given an anticonvulsive drug before the treatment begins.

Generally patients who are properly prepared for the treatments do not dread or despise them. Often they have some temporary disturbance of memory and some physical discomforts. But many times they are greatly relieved of their depression, despair, and sometimes of disturbing thoughts and visions.

Jimmy

Jimmy moved in with me on Monday. Jimmy was about eighteen years old, a tall, olive-complexioned, handsome boy. He said hello in a subdued voice with eyes averted. My attempts to start a conversation were met with polite, but curt responses. After a few days of trying, I gave up any effort to get to know him, and we went on our own ways, wrapped in our own troubles.

Jimmy didn't want to do anything. I mean that literally. It got to be a major job to even get him out of bed. At first simple urging and prodding would do the job, but finally that wouldn't work. A nurse and attendant would pull him out of the bed and help him dress. He wouldn't eat unless someone led him to the table and reminded him to put food in his mouth, chew, and swallow. He simply had to be helped to remember to do everything. He never complained, and he didn't really resist. He was withdrawing further and further from everybody and everything.

I was in my room reading one morning after breakfast. Jimmy was still in bed when the floor nurse came in and tried to get him out of the bed and dressed. This time Jimmy did more than just lie there passively. When she tried to pull the cover back, he grabbed it from her and pulled it up to his chin. He still didn't say anything. The nurse said, "Oh, come on now, Jimmy. You've got to get up." He looked calm and peaceful. She pulled at the cover again. With that, he grabbed her arm and shoved her across the room. She smacked the bathroom door and slid to the floor with a dazed look on her face. Hastily she scrambled up and beat it out of the room. Jimmy closed his eyes and turned over.

In a few moments Dr. Eithman arrived with white coat flapping, followed by the nurse and an attendant. The attendant, John, was a big black guy who was gentle and kind, but strong.

By now I had put my book down and was watching with some concern. Dr. Eithman stood over Jimmy with his arms crossed over his chest. I was interested to see how an experienced psychiatrist would handle this.

"Jimmy," Eithman said, "we will not tolerate this. Get out of that bed." Jimmy didn't budge. "If you can't help yourself, then we'll have to help you." With that, he grabbed Jimmy by the arm and started to pull him up. With unexpected speed Jimmy twirled around on the bed, planted his right foot on Eithman's chest, and gave him a solid kick. Eithman shot across the room, hit the bathroom door, just as the nurse had, and slumped to the floor. Breathing hard now, with a red face, he said, "John, let's get him out of that bed." Both he and John wrapped themselves around Jimmy and tried to get him up.

I don't know how Jimmy did it, but they couldn't budge him from the bed. They strained and grunted and tussled, but they couldn't get him up. Finally Dr. Eithman stood up, puffing with each breath. "Wait here, John. I'll be right back."

In about five minutes he returned with Fred and Bert, two other attendants. The four of them proceeded to try to get Jimmy out of bed. Suddenly Jimmy jumped up screaming and cursing and aiming punches in every direction. I've never seen anybody in such a wild fury. He tore the clothes off of Eithman down to his underwear and shredded the shirts on John and Bert's backs. Of course they were handicapped in restraining him because they were trying not to hurt him. All of them took several good licks before they finally pinned him to the floor.

Eithman shouted to the nurse for a hypodermic of Thorazine. She ran in and poked it into Jimmy's behind while the four men held him down. He was still struggling furiously, and it took all they could do to hold him. After fifteen or twenty minutes it was obvious that he wasn't going to slow down. So they hit him in the rear with another shot. Finally he quit struggling and they loaded him on a stretcher and took him out.

Jimmy was placed in a room with an attendant who stayed with him all the time. His Thorazine dosage was increased to maximum levels. (This information was always available in the ward. Either a talkative nurse or attendant or an overheard conversation provided the latest information.) Finally his panic excitement subsided.

Two days later Jimmy came back, mumbling to himself and walking around in a bemused, drugged fog. Now he was talking, but he made no sense. I went to bed that night a little up tight. Jimmy got in his bed, still muttering to himself.

Something woke me about three in the morning. I looked over at Jimmy's bed where he was sitting up, still talking to himself. This time I could understand him. "My God," he groaned, "blood, nothing but blood all over me. I've killed them all. But they are better off now." He cried and moaned and shook. I got up and walked over to his bed. "Jimmy," I said, "can I help you? What's wrong?" He stuck his arms and legs out toward me. "Look, they are covered with blood; I've killed them all." His hands and feet were covered with brown shoe polish. A can was open on the table near him.

I was chicken. I asked to be moved the next day. I still continued to see Jimmy on the ward and in the dayroom. He was heavily medicated, but now he was moving so fast that one could hardly see him. He ran up and down the hall, scrambled up the fence around the sun porch, and talked at a nonstop rate. After a few weeks he slowed down to a more normal pace and was in a partial release program. But he still had a haunted, hunted look as if he really believed that he had killed somebody. Or as if he was afraid he would.

Faces

3

I WONDER if much of me is reflected in my face? That is, the face my friends see. I look at faces a great deal and carefully. I try to decide what I see there. Perhaps I'm trying to see if my face is mirrored in the faces I look at.

Face watching is an almost compelling pastime in a mental ward. You look at others to see if you can penetrate the outer layers and see the special kind of misery that must lie underneath the mask of each. To understand their predicament might be to know something of your own. And you know that other people are looking at you for the same reasons, and you wonder what your face reflects of you and your life, your misery and your joy.

I sat for an hour or so in the dayroom and looked at faces with a new intensity. I saw a faced etched with the acid of old agony. There were faces hewn from despair, carved from hate, and painted with venom. Many of these faces were softened with pity and compassion. But some were sketched in hate and deceit. Nearly all were unhappy, despairing, alone faces. And they were not all patients' faces either.

Maud

There's the face of Maud. A dark face. A pleasant face. But the pleasantness has smeared and run out of its lines and now it's a flaccid face without vitality, and the pleasantness has merged into resignation. Maud has been chronically and severely depressed for almost three years. Occasionally her features become firm, the lines become sharp, and the basic foundations of her face are strikingly clear. When this happens, the staff watches her closely because she will soon try to kill herself. It's as if the conviction to die lends her face, for a little time, some character and, paradoxically, some life.

Phil

There's Phil's face, smooth, unlined, young as we measure time. His face never had time to show the effects of laughter or joy, or, for that matter, sorrow and forbearance. His struggle was short and violent and fruitless. Now the cares and gains of life will never be reflected in his face. It's locked in frozen timelessness because nothing new or different or happy or sorrowful or painful can ever happen to Phil again. His is a face that is vacuous and empty but without the plasticity or possibility of molding or changing.

Virginia

There is the face of Virginia. It covers two little holes from which a frightened child peers fearfully out at the world. Her mouth turns up at the corners in a pretty little girl's smile, tender and tentative. It is a face that says "please." It's a face that begs for kindness. But from those peepholes, we see the little child, tentative and afraid, who watches everything keenly and sharply, and seems ever vigilant. At the least sign of danger, she runs and hides and drops two small, blank, blue curtains over the peepholes in Virginia's face.

Mac

Not all the interesting faces belong to the patients. If you observe closely and carefully you will see intriguing aspects of the faces of the various staff members. Mac's face was the face of a not too successful but persistent gambler. It was marked across the middle by a pencil line mustache, always sharp and precise. The face was topped by black wavy hair, always neat and well groomed. His face was lined by the ravages of consistently succeeding crises. Crises, I am sure, that were met with aplomb and impassiveness. Mac was an attendant. His personal qualities were paradoxical. He looked like a well-kept ne'er-do-well. But strangely, he had a compassionate quality that was not bred of the need to feed on others' miseries. His compassion seemed to spring from the experience of "having been there." I never asked, and he never said, but I'll bet he had had his days metered with trouble. Probably much of it of his own making.

Miss Wolfe

Miss Wolfe, the head day nurse, had an interesting face too. It was too fat. But not jolly fat. She managed a regular countenance of relative calmness. And I believe that she really believed she was calm. At least about the problems and misery that patients brought to the hospital with them. She showed us a complacent face, but one that was receptive if you didn't demand too much. When you made that mistake, it sort of glazed over and became unfathomable and inscrutable. Her face showed the effects of long years of mastering every situation she confronted. I wonder if she is still mastering them all?

Dr. Vale

Then there was Dr. Vale's face. A boy's face. Topped by a shock of closely clipped hair. He had a petulant, sorrowful look which was often held up by a protruding lower lip. When he came through the ward, his head never turned, his eyes never wavered. He looked straight down at the floor. This kind of stance never provoked much response from his patients. If a particularly desperate one tried to trap him in conversation, he would stop and peer miserably at the floor and mumble unintelligibly until he could escape. I always had the feeling that he was being pursued by a bill collector from a loan company. His face had a sort of harassed, haunted quality. At times it would light up. And when it did, it was a joy to see. I guess this was mainly because it was so unexpected. Like seeing someone hit his thumb with a hammer and then laugh rather than cry.

Sue

Sue was a ward nurse. She was a young girl whose cute figure was always in motion. You couldn't get a good perspective of her face because it was constantly jarred by her mouth, which was frantically chomping on chewing gum all the time. You couldn't talk to Sue. You could talk at her, but she usually didn't hear. She was preoccupied with thoughts of that last weekend at the beach, or maybe next weekend at the beach. While you tried to talk to her, those busy little eyes would be searching and seeking. If they spotted Dr. Vale or another male staff member, you knew to stand aside because she was going to be moving. Once she approached me with my prescribed morning pill. "Miss Wolfe has already given me two of those," I said just for the hell of it. She snapped her Juicy Fruit three or four times in rapid succession, looked around the dayroom quickly, and finally she said, "Here, take this." And away she went. I could have had a grapefruit in my mouth and she would never have known it.

What do they see?

I wondered as I looked at everyone else, "What do you see in my face? Does it show the careless disregard that Sue's face shows? The careful obsessive mastery of Miss Wolfe's, or the impatient guilt of Dr. Vale's?" Perhaps, I thought, they saw the bland impassiveness of Phil's face; a face that no longer mirrors Phil's engagement in what for him is life. Maybe they saw some of the misery of Maud's face, a face that looked in hell and was forever scarred by the burning fire.

So, I look in the mirror of others' faces. And I see something of myself in every face I see. Misery, joy, despair, hope, anger, and compassion—all of these and more. So I can't be certain about what I see when I look at you. Is it you I see or just a part of me that's reflected there?

I look in a conventional glass mirror. Just as everybody else. And I see a friend, and an enemy, and I see a stranger. There's a man who looks pretty calm. Really, rather impassive. Not bad looking, perhaps a bit fleshy. His nose is a little big. The kind of face that looks pretty tough unless it's well shaved and washed and rested. He looks a bit stern and not approachable. Is he unfriendly? Does he have such important things to do that he had rather you didn't bother him? That's some of what I see. But that's not what is really there.

What this face is masking is a trembling fear. Fear that is all the more fearful because it has no relevant danger to attach itself to. It's fear in search of an object. It's fear that has become so generalized that the sound of any affective "bell" causes uncontrollable panic which that face must try to hide. This face must remain impassive. It can't risk the luxury of sagging unconcern and passiveness. It might never regain its casted features. It's a face that covers fear, hate, despair, and resentment. But it's a face that also covers a tentative hope to be a "person," a need to be relied on, a prayer to be succored, a wish to be open to others, and to give of itself.

Well, the devil with it! I'm going to have to give up my hobby of face watching. After all, when I look at you I don't know any more than before. Do I see you or me? Do I see what you are or what you want to be? Do I see myself and you in an inextricable conglomeration of projected hopes and fears, or do I just see what I have to see?

Hal

Hal's long arms dangled listlessly at his sides; his hands were flaccid and lifeless. When he moved, he looked as if he wouldn't make it to his next appointed stop. When he spoke, his voice shook and his tone was so soft you could hardly understand him. He would spend hours working on a picture puzzle in the dayroom. Sometimes, when frustrated, he would scatter pieces over the floor and amble away.

Hal was a second year student in the medical school. He was humiliated to be a patient on the psychiatric ward of the hospital which housed his school. He dreaded seeing his fellow students when they came by to serve a few days on the floor. Hal had been in psychotherapy with Dr. Eithman, one of the staff psychiatrists, for several months before he was admitted as an inpatient. Someone told me that he had taken a room in a local motel and had called Dr. Eithman one night and threatened to kill himself. Eithman persuaded him to come to the hospital instead.

All Hal could talk about was the shame his parents must feel over his collapse, and how he had let them down. He told me of his overwhelming attacks of depression and how he would cry for hours and be unable to sleep or eat for days. He was afraid to go back to school but too ashamed not to try.

Even though he told me of his hurting and his distress, he was curiously detached, as if he were talking about a friend rather than himself. And even though he talked about these problems, he was guarded in revealing himself. He never talked about how he felt, or what he thought now, or what or whom he liked now. He always talked about the past or the future. And he always discussed himself in dispassionate, unemotional, objective terms. It's as if he were discussing the problems of one of the patients he someday hoped to have. He was quietly friendly but subtly removed. He was involved, but not all the way. He participated but never gave. In short, he was like a man treading water. He was getting nowhere, but at least he was not drowning. And you had the feeling that if someone pulled him out and dried him off, he would later refuse to take swimming lessons. He had to fail somehow. With quiet determination, his every action seemed to say, "I will not win."

In a few weeks, he was released from the unit and went back to school. After a month more, he was readmitted to the ward in a deeply depressed state. He would not talk or eat. In the early morning he would come to the dayroom, sit in a chair and remain there all day, never talking or reading, with his eyes half closed and with a sad, drawn face.

One day he was gone. I asked John, an attendant, where he was, and John said that his family had had him released. They had taken him to a private psychiatric hospital somewhere else. I felt sorry for Hal and uncomfortably pessimistic for his future.

Some of my friends

Phil was probably the most typical example of what most people expect when they hear the term "mental illness" or "emotional disorder," or "crazy." He was seemingly happy and unperturbed, and very much out of it. He often talked to people whom you couldn't see. Sometimes the conversation would amuse him, and he would chuckle and smile. You could seldom understand what he was talking about or to whom. If you asked him, he would just smile shyly in a vague and detached way. But he usually wouldn't answer. Phil couldn't sustain a conversation for any length of time. If you asked what he was doing, he would reply briefly, "I'm listening to a record." Which he was. Or "I'm reading the newspaper." Which he was. He wasn't impolite. It was just obvious that he was preoccupied and busy with other things. He was a fine looking young man of twenty-three. Cleanly featured with dark wavy hair and an olive complexion. But his mind had surrendered. You had the feeling that he had ceased to struggle. He had found a way to avoid the pain and his mind wasn't about to risk another bout with it. Because this behavior resulted in some small degree of comfort, there was little hope for any real creative struggle from him. I don't know what eventually happened to Phil. He went to a state mental hospital finally. But I'll bet wherever he is today, he is still talking to his unseen friends, and he is smiling and chuckling and gone from our world.

I mention Phil to provide a contrast between the popular

stereotype of mental disorder (which he typifies), and the real model of aberration which is so much more frequent and much messier.

Liz, I think, will give you a picture of what occurs more frequently. She walked around the ward and dayroom all day long, never resting. Sometimes she would cry softly, but most of the time she just seemed worried and agitated. She looked through you unseeingly, as if she were searching for something that was always just beyond her sight. Sometimes, she staggered as if drunk or dizzy. Occasionally, she walked blindly into a chair or table.

Liz was a small, rather homely brunette. She was about thirty years old when I knew her. Part of her trouble was arsenic. She had eaten a package of rat poison and had spent several days hooked up to an artificial kidney and various other devices. One of her two kids had found her on the kitchen floor and had called daddy to come home. One of her fellow patients asked her one day why she had taken the rat poison. Liz looked blank and then inquired softly, "What else could I do?" Somehow, we knew what she meant.

After two or three months, under rather heavy medication, she calmed down a bit and went home. But she had a driven look on her face when she left. It made you wonder where she would find the strength she would need when the black cloak of despair fell on her again. I never heard from her again.

Betty usually sat on a sofa in the dayroom of the ward. Her face was a study in despair. She was about thirty-five years old. She was somewhat pretty in a harassed, tired sort of way. But she sat on the sofa all day long for weeks, never initiating a conversation with anyone, but answering briefly and courteously when addressed.

One day I sat down near her. Finally, after a few moments

of uncomfortable silence, I ventured hesitantly, "Hi, Betty. It looks cold outside, doesn't it?" She looked at me in a weary but kind way. And she gave me a brief, tiny smile. But she didn't speak. She never did speak, at least not that day. I tried a few brief remarks. And she wasn't rude and didn't appear annoyed, but she wouldn't talk to me.

A few days later while sitting in the dayroom, I heard a scream. No, it was more like a wailing gargle. It lasted for several long minutes. I learned later that Betty had broken a mirror in her compact and had tried to cut her wrists. She wasn't screaming about the pain. She was screaming in her frustration at having been stopped before she could kill herself.

After three months, she was given a series of electric shock treatments. She improved rapidly and began to talk and eat. Things she had done seldom in the past.

Her mood improved with shock treatments and with it her appetite and her ability to interact with those around her. And apparently she was able to derive some satisfaction from life. Her husband came to see her one day and decided to take her home. This he did against her wishes and the wishes of her doctor.

I didn't hear from her for a few weeks. Then one day in a psychotherapy session I remarked casually that it was heartening for me to see someone as depressed as Betty get to feeling so much better and finally go home.

My therapist looked at me somewhat suspiciously and with a grimace of pain said, "Then you don't know what happened?" "No," I answered, "I don't know what happened. So what happened?" His reply was labored. "Her husband beat her up the night she got home. She went into the bathroom, locked the door, and cut her throat with a razor blade. She's dead."

If you are going to shock people back to life, you should

be reasonably certain that they are going to be better off than they were when they were "dead."

One man's struggle

Dr. Trempton was a new patient on the ward. With anxious, quick, hyperalert moves he responded to everything and everyone around him. He was obviously distressed and anxious. His hands trembled and his voice cracked a bit when he tried to carry on a conversation. His face had a tired, harassed, chronically worried expression like a fox at the end of the hunting season. But he was friendly and obviously tried to show his concern for those with problems around him.

In spite of his attempts to be one of us, he really couldn't relax his "doctor" posture. He dressed every morning in his conservative suit with his conservative tie, and he maintained this dress all day, even in the recreation periods. He was always on stage, always talking to his "patients," always formal, always anxious to maintain a soft but firm barrier between himself and the rest of the world. He was the kind of man who would call his wife Mrs. Trempton, and by golly, he really did! Even more to my surprise, she called him "Dr. Trempton." They had three grown children, and I often wondered how they managed to be conceived! How do you get around to the topic of the possibility of sexual intercourse with someone whom you refer to, and think of, as Mrs.?

After a few days, Dr. Trempton's need to maintain his distance became more pronounced. I noticed that when someone talked to him, he would back away from him, trying to keep a suitable space between himself and whoever had accosted him. Sometimes it was almost ludicrous to watch an eager chatterbox backing Dr. T. across the dayroom at a near trot. When he finally collided with the wall, he would slither quickly along it with rapid crablike moves until he finally escaped his pursuer. If somebody sat down near him, he got up and walked away.

Finally one morning I saw him standing in the hall, not moving a muscle. I knew something was wrong because he had on a bathrobe and slippers rather than his suit. As I approached him, I could see that he was locked in such a rigid stance that his whole body was shaking.

"Don't come near me," he moaned. "Keep everyone away from me. I am rotten. My body has rotted and I will infect you if you touch me. My God, I smell putrid; horrible. I stink. I am made of corruption and feces." He cried and moaned and shook as he stood in rigid attention. His eyes stared straight ahead, never blinking or focusing.

He was so dramatically convincing that I almost jumped away to keep from being infected. Then I felt the first inkling of an unpleasant smell rising to my consciousness, and I got out!

For days and days Dr. T. shook and cried and begged everyone to keep away from him. The nearer anyone got to him, the more miserable he became. He maintained that his body had rotted and that he would infect anyone who touched him. His face was a continued study in mortal fear and terror.

In our group sessions, he pulled his chair as far away from the others as possible and sat facing the wall, eyes alert, crying "Don't touch me" at frequent intervals. We had no success in reassuring him. After a hundred choruses of "You're not rotten. You don't smell bad. You won't infect anyone," we gave up and let him moan in the corner.

We had three group sessions each week. There were eight people in our group, which was led by Dr. Barlow, a psychiatrist. He tried everything he knew to involve Dr. Trempton. Several sessions were devoted to a discussion of Dr. Trempton and his behavior, and why he felt the way he did. All of this with the poor man sitting and moaning in the corner. But now, his situation was getting to be life threatening.

Dr. Trempton finally made the obvious logical deduction that since his body was dead and rotted, it of course needed no nourishment. Now he was refusing to eat, and after several days he was not eating voluntarily at all. At intervals he was being fed by a nose tube to the stomach. Clearly, however, this was not satisfactory, because after several weeks of this he had lost a great deal of weight; his cheeks were sunken and hollow, and his eyes seemed to be falling into his brain.

We tried to help him in our group. We talked to him and about him. We tried every argument and every subtlety to get him involved with us in some way. We tried ridicule, humor, threats, and intimidation. Nothing worked. When somebody physically approached him, he would scream and cry and run around the room in agitation, finally frightening everyone away.

One day in our group Carl exhausted his patience. Carl was a big, husky, paranoid guy. He thought that the Mafia was out to get him. (Maybe he wasn't crazy at all!) Anyway, Carl got fed up one day as Dr. Trempton was begging him, "Don't touch me; I'm rotten."

"The hell with that crazy crap," Carl yelled, his patience gone. With that he grabbed Dr. T. in a bear hug and held on.

"I've got you and you're not rotten, and I won't let go," panted Carl as Dr. Trempton struggled violently to break away. He screamed and cried and begged Carl to let him go.

We looked questioningly at Dr. Barlow. He just shook his head, and we all sat there watching Carl struggle with Dr. Trempton's life.

The struggle went on for hours, I thought. I looked at my watch. Thirty minutes had passed. With a last groan and a final struggle, Dr. Trempton collapsed and lay in Carl's arms, crying quietly. After a while Carl helped him up and took him to his room.

After that, Dr. Trempton's delusions and panic began to subside. He was fearful at first, but he managed to sit with us in our group meetings, and finally he began to eat with others of us at the dining table. The aloof distance between himself and others began to dissolve, and in a few more weeks he was slapping friends on the back and calling others by their first name. I knew he was on his way out when I heard him refer to his wife as "Nancy."

Cured?

4

DAYS PLOD BY. Have I been in this place only a week? Have I ever been anywhere else? Already the days and nights have become depressingly predictable. They are anesthetizingly the same.

I awake with a vague awareness of myself, followed quickly by anxiety and nausea. Another precious day had been lost and nothing gained. Soon the nurse comes by. In her impersonal detached way she asks, "How do we feel this morning?" She means well, but she doesn't hear my answer, or she doesn't like my answer. So after a few days I quit answering. They probably note on my chart, "sullen, withdrawn, and flattened affect." She pops a pill in my mouth (a stimulant), I close my eyes again, and gradually the nausea subsides.

Out of the bed, slowly, numbly, leadenly. To the bathroom where I try not to look at myself, and then on to breakfast. Various patients and staff sit around the dining room (which is also the dayroom). They are drinking coffee, smoking cigarettes, crying, or sometimes eating. Finally, that's over. Back to the room; make up the bed. (This is good therapy.) Then we wait.

Depending on the day, we may bunch up and descend to the ground floor to the workshop. Here a crafts teacher (occupational therapist) does her earnest best to convince us it is dignified and adult to aspire to, and actually make, a beaded wallet or a potholder or a looped belt.

Occupational therapists believe in what they are doing. Books have been written and college courses taught that deal exclusively and exhaustively with the therapeutic possibilities of arts and crafts. In my opinion, any activity must be intrinsically worthwhile before it can have therapeutic possibilities. Frivolous activities are worthwhile, but not when they are compelled to travel under the guise of serious and profound import. There's nothing wrong with frivolous occupation of one's time. But not everyone takes it seriously when he builds a lamp or an ashtray. Occupational therapists, though, seem to regard these "beading" sessions as seriously as if one were building a digital computer. The condescension involved in praising a grown man or woman for a childish task is demeaning to those who do it and to those to whom it is done.

The causes of most emotional disorders are generally unknown. If you doubt this, observe the "treatment" in an up-to-date psychiatric facility. There are drugs, lectures, soul searching (religious therapy), social participation, arts and crafts, electric shock, milieu therapy, music therapy, psychotherapy; all of these things and others (there's even garden therapy) are thrown at the poor patient. The apparent hope is that something will help. That's not so bad. The goal is desirable and valid. But, oh my, the defensiveness of most psychiatrists and many psychologists. Almost without exception, they bow to analytic theory, and their chant is "the inhibition of instinctive drives and the resulting conflict." In a nutshell, that's their explanation for the "functional" mental aberrations. They may object to my superficial statement. But, in defense, their lengthy explanations always boil down to "repressed conflicts." Well, okay, repressed conflicts it is. Then how do you resolve them? Their answer is usually psychotherapy. This I can accept, even though as a treatment method it is costly, inefficient, and too often ineffective. But psychotherapy by whom? By a resident physician in training, or a fourth year medical student, or a third year nurse, or perhaps the clinical psychology intern who is grudgingly permitted to hang around? I don't believe that psychiatrists who have completed their training ever do individual psychotherapy in the hospital setting. But they supervise medical students and interns who are trying to do this. (Actually, residents in training are the only ones who have formal sessions; I have overdrawn the point to a degree.) I must admit that they probably do little actual harm, but they don't do a hell of a lot of good either.

I am sure that there must be swank psychiatric hospitals where you get psychotherapy from an eminently qualified person. But you'd better not be mentally ill and poor. That's a deadly combination. And it's even tougher if you're unattractive and semiliterate.

Perhaps the methods of psychotherapy can someday be openly employed by other professional groups who have sufficient and appropriate training. There is little in medical training that is even nearly appropriate to the employment of the technique. But it is often jealously guarded by some as a medical prerogative even when the masses are crying for help.

The routine

When we are through with our two hour "beading" session, we head back to the ward. There are some patients still back on the ward doing their "beading" there. They are too sick to leave. And we patients who go down to the first floor look down on those who stay behind. We have our own little caste system, yet the pecking order doesn't necessarily rest on degrees of sickness. The key to high status seems to be unusual emotional liability. You must be occasionally lucid and even bright and sharp. But if that's what you are always, you have little social value. However, if you're often bright and alert, and sometimes depressed and preferably hallucinating, you are high on the scale of "valued" patients. You can use a little violence to increase your value. But you have to be careful here. Too much or too often will get you restraint and isolation, or, if you persist, the state hospital.

If it's one of three therapy days out of the week, I meet my psychiatrist for about thirty minutes. I look forward to this with hope. Maybe today something will happen. Maybe I'll do something. Maybe he will. I am disappointed one more time.

If you go to a teaching hospital, your therapist is likely to be a young physician who has completed his medical training and his internship and is now serving an apprenticeship in a psychiatric setting. Such trainees are called residents. You may be his first psychotherapy patient if he is a beginning first-year resident. If you are fortunate enough to get a resident in his final year, the third, he will have had a fair amount of experience.

My session with him may be helpful if he is far enough along in his training, if he is not preoccupied with whether or not I am trying to manipulate him, or if he is not too concerned about revealing his own hostility or anxiety. But he *is* a learner. I am his subject matter. This might be quite an interesting arrangement if I weren't spending all of my money and much of my energy, and if I weren't desperately afraid that I might never recover.

Dr. Vale sticks his head out of his office; he mumbles something while looking miserably at the floor. Since I'm scheduled for this time, I assume that it's my name he called, and I walk into the tiny office. It's not his office exclusively. Rather, it's one of those small, impersonal cubicles used by various staff members.

I sit down, and Dr. Vale in his white coat with clipboard in hand looks expectantly at me, pen poised.

"God," I say, "I just feel like hell. I have absolutely no energy. I feel drained. Empty. Sick."

His pen flies over the pad on the clipboard. Rather startled I wonder, "What the hell did I say?" No verbal response from Dr. Vale. He's caught up now with his writing, and he again cocks his eyebrows at me in anticipation.

As if on cue, I respond, "All I can think of is how afraid and lonely I feel. I just feel sick at my stomach all the time. I can never relax. I worry all the time if I can ever learn somehow to live with myself."

Dr. Vale's pen leaps to life again, and he writes furiously, trying to see his pad through the smoke of the cigarette dangling from a corner of his mouth. Finally it looks as if he's caught up, and I begin again. Actually, you can't say a great deal in just thirty minutes when your therapist is recording your words in longhand! After our fits and starts of words and notes, our session is nearly over. I'm talking now about the tension and pressure I feel. "Sometimes," I say, "I feel as if it will build and build until I'll explode."

"Well," Dr. Vale responds (which takes me by surprise since he seldom says anything), "don't do it here." He stands up, signaling that the session is ended.

Another session is over. He has another pad full of notes. No doubt he will describe to his therapy supervisor the things I said which exemplify my "resistance," or my "ego strength," or lack thereof; or my "phallic envy," or "anal complex," or what have you. Then they probably become engrossed in a psychological postmortem. Meanwhile the "corpse" reports to the ward dining room for lunch, which he can't eat because he's still nauseated.

Meals are usually pretty grim. There is little of the happy social banter which accompanies most group meals. Then too, there's not much appetite either. Sometimes there's an exception. Today, George, a graduate biologist, is manic. He's shoveling food into his mouth, gulping it down, meanwhile humming and singing and swaying from side to side. His nose starts to bleed, but he eats on, oblivious. His deliriously "happy" torment is painful to see. He will leave the hospital in a few weeks "improved." But in two months he will take a massive dose of insect poison and die alone in the woods. He will be missing for weeks before his body is found.

I get up from the table and go back to the room. I wasn't hungry anyway.

Another round-up after lunch. Everybody in the film room. Today we see Mildred. She has a stomachache. Every time her work gets stressful or things go wrong, Mildred's stomach hurts. Then a flashback. We see Mildred as a little girl. She is with her young sister, Babs, who takes Mildred's toys away from her, spits on her, kicks her, and generally makes her life miserable. But when Mildred finally gets fed up and smashes Babs, her mother (watch it here, girls!) rushes in and tells her that she is mean and ungrateful, and hints darkly that mother won't love her if she beats hell out of sister. Of course, that's it for Mildred.

Now she is grown up, and every time she has to cope with an authority figure (mother), she becomes fearful (stomachache) that she will be a failure (lose mother's love). So then we all exclaim in wonder. Mildred is reacting to a childhood pattern of experiences. Her fear over the potential loss of love (and hence physical life itself) causes anxiety, resulting in a cramped stomach for Mildred. All very good, and clear, except it doesn't seem to have much bearing on our stomachs. We didn't have a sister. Or, if we did, mother hated her too.

We exchange wise observations on how powerful childhood emotional experiences are, and we troop back to the ward. Meanwhile the psychiatrist who is leading the group discussion departs with a satisfied expression on his face. He has helped us develop "insight," he thinks. Big deal. About all the poor patients get from this experience is some little notice, greatly diluted, from someone (father) who has the ability to solve problems (magic). Anyhow, our stomachs still hurt and no doubt, so does poor, persecuted Mildred's.

A couple of days a week you are in a group therapy session. But you still just talk about *things.* And I mean "talk" in the most superficial meaning of the word. You talk about how you feel, how you feel about someone else in the group, how you think they feel about you. You try and try. And sometimes you get tired of talking. So you just sit and try to endure it. If you question this "therapy," you will be told, "Because of the composition of the group, we have limited goals for it." The white coat has spoken.

I think the basic fallacy with the techniques of psychotherapy that have "limited goals" is that they deal with the product and not the process. You trot out your anger, fear, hostility, and other noxious emotions, and you examine and talk "about" all of these feelings. But you don't actually undergo the emotional experience of feeling these things. Real sessions of therapy must engender fear, hostility, love, hope, despair, and all the other feelings that make us human, and, sadly, sometimes only humanoid. The sessions should have as their purpose the *experiencing* of the emotion, not the discussion of the experiencing of the emotion. I hope the reader sees the obvious but vital difference between these two circumstances. This, of course, is not a new idea at all. It's as old as the talking therapies themselves. But all too often this gross difference is subtly ignored, and the discussion of the feeling is substituted for the experience of the feeling itself. The measure of this distinction is analogous to talking about making love to Sophia Loren and making love to Sophia Loren.

So dinner time finally comes along. Back to the tasteless meal (not the cook's fault) and the growing realization that another day has almost slipped away.

After dinner a few visitors come along. Most of them look uncomfortable. They glance covertly from the corner of their eyes, apparently expecting some wild, slobbering maniac to spring on them at any moment. People sit in pairs or small groups and talk. Two fellows play ping pong. There's a bridge game underway and two or three people are reading. A pastoral, serene scene, almost.

Bill is still talking softly to himself over in the corner. And you can tell by his manner that occasionally someone answers. Tom tries to talk to you for a minute, but he's so anxious that he's doing a soft shoe routine and he forgets what he was trying to tell you and wanders away looking for something he can't seem to find. Far away, down the long corridor, you can hear an occasional muffled scream.

After awhile

After three or four weeks in the hospital, I seemed to calm down a bit. At least I wasn't visibly shaking. My bewilderment was still great. I couldn't believe that this was me in a ward of "crazy" people. There was old Mrs. Gold. She was constantly trying to sneak out of the hospital and catch a bus to Dallas. Why, nobody knows. She has never lived there. She even made it once to the bus station, and got on the right bus. But she was caught before it got underway.

Can I be as sick as they are? Mrs. Gold, for instance, doesn't know why she's in the hospital, or even where she is. Lately she has begun to call us by some new names. We have concluded that she was using her children's and friends' names. Occasionally she will go for three or four days without eating. I haven't seen anybody come to visit her. I guess somebody somewhere is paying the bill, though.

Then there's old Mr. Jump. The rumor is that the old man is a millionaire. He founded a food processing company that now specializes in various kinds of meat products. The brand name of his foods was familiar to me. The old man will sit in the dayroom and talk incessantly about "going to the bathroom." He tries to go about every two or three minutes, all day long. One attendant has to stay with him all the time to keep him from injuring himself. I wonder what will happen to him when his family gets tired of spending *his* money on him and sends him to the state mental hospital? You can bet that they won't have someone sitting with him all day. The poor man is so agitated and upset that he complains and cries and moans all day long. Everybody on the ward is concerned.

See evil, hear evil

The paranoids among us are the most interesting, and, in some ways, the most intact of the lot. I'm sure that you could gather a group of mental patients together at random, and you would be able to pick the paranoids by appearance alone. At least this is true in the early stage of their disturbance. Usually in apparently good physical condition, they look acutely alert, wary, and suspicious. Remember when you brought your date home at three in the morning? If you can recall how her father looked at you, you will have some inkling of what I mean.

Bill would soon leave the hospital. Forever, I hope. He had been paranoid. He was a young, personable man; a college graduate who was a field engineer for the telephone company. We talked a lot together, and he told me what had happened to him.

Bill had become suspicious that his colleagues and supervisors were plotting against him. They had started out just simply disliking him, so he thought. But soon they were planning to fire him. Finally he became convinced that they were going to kill him.

One day, he said, he got a pistol and took it to work with him. During his lunch hour (he was careful not to use company time) he went in to see his boss. He demanded to know why everybody hated him, and he showed his boss the gun, and told him that he was prepared if any of them tried to get him.

He must have had an understanding boss. Bill said that he was told to take a week off and come to the hospital to see a psychiatrist. Bill was agreeable to this, he said, since he had no fear that they would find anything but the "truth," that his associates were out to get him.

I asked Bill what the psychiatrist had told him. "Well," he said thoughtfully, "he told me that I was sick, and that I might spend the rest of my life in a mental hospital if I didn't get treatment now."

I was curious: "How did that strike you?" He paused for a moment. "You know," he said, "somehow I knew something was wrong. So I decided to come here for a few days." "How do you feel now?" I asked. "Do you still believe that they are plotting to kill you?" He answered promptly, "No, and I don't know why I felt that way in the first place."

Bill was essentially recovered. But he still harbored some reservations. I could tell by his resistant manner that he still was trying to make an irrational experience rational.

Some of my fellow patients wouldn't talk at all about their fears and suspicions. Some, like Sue, had accepted the fact that nobody else believed their stories, but like her they hadn't been able to give them up themselves. She told me one day, "I know that nobody believes that the FBI is bugging my telephone. And I don't intend to say any more about it. But I know damn well that they are doing it."

True to her word, she said nothing more about it. And if anyone asked, she would smile and say, "I know that was silly. I don't know how I ever came to believe it." In a few weeks, she went home, probably still convinced that the FBI was listening to her telephone conversations. In view of recent events, I wonder if they were.

Although I was still depressed and miserable and couldn't eat much or sleep, I wasn't interesting enough or obviously "crazy" enough to fit in well. Attendants and nurses drifted in to work, and in a few weeks most were gone. Frequently, the least tactful ones would say, in effect, "What are you doing here? You don't look nutty."

Far from pleasing me, not only did this kind of remark seem presumptuous and prying, but it seemed to imply that I was taking a rather unusual vacation. At first, I would try to explain how I felt and why I needed treatment. But this obviously bored them. Nothing is so depressing as depression. Finally one middle-aged nurse's aide asked me what I was doing here. I told her that I was a sex maniac and that I had raped twelve women. I told her that I couldn't control myself and that I might go berserk at any moment. She hastened to put some distance between us. Although I am sure she read my record and found out I was lying, she regarded me with respect for the rest of her stay there.

The physician patients among us usually were there because of drugs. At least that's what they would say. This must have been harder on them than it was on any other professional person who was a patient. They were so accustomed to maintaining a Godlike stance that it must have been tough to be reduced to the status of not just patient, but a mental patient, which is a considerably lower status (even among mental patients!)

There is enough anguish and misery on a ward of mental patients for the most practiced sadist. There are physically recovering suicides. There are women who can't care for their families and are worried about what may be happening to their children. There are men who have lost their chance at a decent livelihood and who know that a few weeks or maybe months in a hospital will bankrupt them. There are those who are harassed and tortured, night and day, by voices others cannot hear. There are people who feel so miserable and sad, and they may not know why, that they would rather be dead. And there are those who hate themselves and the rest of the world so much that they can find no solace or love or compassion or peace. Indeed, they can't even accept what is freely given. All in all, this is not a promising place to try to regain your own humanity.

Who's sick?

I have come to know that this little group of miseries is just a small sample of the burdens that people everywhere carry with them. All desperate people are not in a hospital somewhere. In fact, few are.

I seemed to be losing my humanness. After my initial gain, I went downhill rapidly. I was periodically seized by unexplainable, unexpected, and violent panics. I couldn't anticipate them, much less understand them. I spent hundreds of hours going over and over my life, trying to find the "magic" moment when it went bad. I guess everyone who has been in this kind of situation tries to reduce it to simple terms. We try to discover the traumatizing instant—the one thing that caused it all.

Perhaps it happened when dad caught me behind the bed with my cousin Sally, engaged in anatomical research!? Maybe it was the time I killed the cat with my new bow and arrow set? Or was it when I flunked arithmetic in the fourth grade and mother cried? Maybe it was because dad was absent from home often, and I didn't get proper fatherly love? Maybe my dependency needs were never satisfied? Maybe I repress all my hostility toward authority figures? Could it be that I have a thyroid deficiency or perhaps a brain tumor?

You are compelled to search for simple, understandable causes. And you believe that if you ever understand and find those causes, you will be okay. But like most of those things we wish were simple, it isn't.

I came to understand myself (I use this word in its most restricted sense) more and more. I believe that I could write an exhaustive, responsible, and objective account of my psyche. How it came to be and its major dimensions and characteristics. I even believe that I could present a pretty fair psychodynamic account of my major personality conflicts and difficulties. But all this avails me little. Now, I am just a knowledgeable, miserable struggler. The only thing that has been added to that statement is "knowledgeable." Just as the biochemist describes the division of cancer cells and is powerless to intervene in the process, so I was unable to stop the malignant growth of my "cancer." It mattered little that I had a pretty thorough understanding of what the process entailed.

But this is an almost unavoidable paradox. You are compelled to think about yourself and your behavior in psychological terms. But this very understanding gets in the way of benign, remedial growth. The probing and understanding can become itself a part of the disease, perhaps even more debilitating then the original complaint.

As the days and weeks went by, my knowledge of myself and my problems increased. Concurrently, my depression was increasing. The days blended one into another in a dull, gray morass of monotonous inertia. My clarity in beginning to see myself was matched by a concomitant deterioration in my ability to cope with what I saw. Weeks became months, and as I began to realize how little I had accomplished in my grasping efforts to regain control of myself, I was embittered and discouraged. Now I had a new set of problems to cope with. At this point, I was struggling with the hospitalization syndrome. My initiative and what little drive I had left were consumed in becoming a product of the ward routine. The mechanics of bathing, dressing, eating, reporting to the various activities, and ostensibly participating in the group and individual therapy sessions became ends in themselves. To cope with the regime was now my goal.

So, slowly but perceptibly, I went downhill. Four months after I entered the hospital, I was more depressed and anxious than I had been upon entering. Analysts will explain this as treatment regression. An expected development. I am in no position to argue this point, although it smacks of rationalization to me. At any rate, I felt worse, however you explain it. I had spent all of the money we had and put us in hock for some years to come. I had been unable to take a good job offer from a university that came about a month after I came into the hospital. And I didn't know if I would be permitted to complete my degree when and if I was able.

Giving up

I had just about given up hope of ever enjoying anything in life again. I had almost resigned myself to losing my wife and our life together. After all, how long could she wait for her life to resume? I was preparing myself for transfer to a state mental hospital, although I was sure that I would not endure this forever. I had made up my mind that at some point I would kill myself rather than face an eternity of anguish. I just hadn't yet decided when I was going to finally and irrevocably abandon all hope. Is this the kind of surrender that's necessary for psychological victory? Christ said that you must give up your life to save it. Does this spiritual concept carry an analogous psychological parallel? It might. Because, for me, the virtual abandonment of hope left space for something to grow.

Slowly and almost imperceptively, I began to feel better. I cannot account for the change. It may have been the antidepressant medication. Maybe it was some gain from psychotherapy. Or it may be that I just wore my depression down. The more likely answer is that it was the interaction of all these things that made the difference. At any rate, there was no burst of insight or blinding moment of revelation, no sublime conversion, or any of the other magical moments we hope for. It was just slow, grinding work.

I came to regard the pathology I was experiencing as really not a part of me. (Of course, there are sound psychological reasons why one would do this.) I came to see "it" as my adversary. And a struggle began between "it" and "me" for dominance of the person I had come to know as RH. This tactical change in strategy (not consciously deliberate, I can assure you) enabled me to use one facet of my character to advantage—stubbornness. This kind of attitudinal shift then made my personality liability of stubbornness into an asset. I now felt that I would hold out longer than "it" could. This is the only time in my life that I was able to make my rigidity and inflexibility useful.

As I've said, there was not a sudden burst of psychological insight, no glorious peak of experience, no sudden cataclysmic freedom. One day I just had several moments of calmness, of freedom from anxiety and despair. Then there were even times when an incident seemed funny to me. There were a few more moments when I dared hope that I would live normally again. I was almost afraid to think about it since my hopes had been crushed so often before.

A person who hasn't lived with continuous anxiety and fear probably cannot fully appreciate what it means to have a few moments of peace. It is so sweet. You guard those moments alone, until you feel you have enough to share them with someone else.

Then (this is included as information for the clinicians among you), I began to sleep a little better. And on occasion, I even enjoyed something I ate. I started slowly to gain back a little of the twenty-five or so pounds I had lost. I began to think a little of my schooling and to plan on going back to work on my dissertation. I also worried about acceptance or rejection when I asked to be readmitted to candidacy at the university. I started to see my wife, Nancy, as an attractive and desirable woman again instead of as a shoulder to cry on or as a symbol of silent reproach.

All of this came slowly. I was almost afraid to tell Nancy that I felt better. I was fearful that it wouldn't last. But I was better, and I felt better. Soon I started to plan on leaving the hospital; I would go part-time at first and then forever, I hoped. Finally, I did leave, in mortal fear that I might have to return. I was very shaky, unsure of myself and quite irritable and nasty. I went home with my wife one afternoon with my heart in my mouth. Since that day, we have struggled together.

Loneliness and belonging

5

MY DEPARTURE from the hospital was accomplished with feelings of hope and anticipation, overlaid with fear. My initial decline had happened so quickly and so unexpectedly that I was in constant fear that it might happen again.

I was accepted back into the doctoral program at the university, and shortly thereafter I was offered a job as a psychologist at a residential treatment center for handicapped children. As time passed I began to regain some confidence, to enjoy living again. My dissertation topic had been accepted at the university, and I was busy trying to bring it together for final writing. At the same time I was working at the center evaluating children, consulting with parents and teachers and beginning to learn something of therapy with disturbed and cerebrally damaged children.

Though I was working productively and learning new skills, I was still periodically assailed by attacks of anxiety, depression, and lethargy. The attacks came without warning and without apparent precipitating causes. I still suffered the fear of again failing to keep my equilibrium, of again losing my ability to be a responsible, productive human being. But I also began to realize that I had to make what I could of myself by myself. The conviction was developing for me that, although I could hope for, and get, help and support, I had to do for myself. The loneliness, spawned by the knowledge that independence can be achieved only by acting and being responsible for oneself, threatened my growth. To begin to appreciate what it really means to be alone is to begin to see the possibilities inherent in living or dying. The paradox of my struggle focused around my panic over my feelings of abandonment and loneliness, and my anxiety and fear of meaningful relationships! Loneliness and belonging are really the same problem or task viewed from two different perspectives.

To be alone

I think something like this must have happened at one time or another to everyone. You're in bed at night with the lights out waiting to go to sleep. You are casting mentally about in a rather aimless fashion when at the edge of awareness you become sensitive to some uneasy feeling. As you begin to look at the feeling, to try to make something of it, you become aware that it is a feeling of loneliness, a distasteful solitude. You come to realize that it's not just a feeling of restlessness from boredom and inactivity; it's your first real confrontation with the primary "curse" of the human condition: "self-awareness" and "dreadful freedom."

This is a profound, and, for most, a decidedly uncomfortable realization. At this point most of us push the feeling away and deliberately begin to think of more bearable things: how we are going to pay the house note, whether we should buy a washing machine, or what we are going to say to the first guy who gives us some lip in the conference tomorrow. But usually we can only stall for time. The feeling and the thought will persist, and some night we must deliberately confront them.

When I examine this feeling closely, I find three things with which I must deal. One of them is that my life, what it is and what it is to be, is my responsibility. It is not the sum of the products of chance and heredity plus how I happen to have been treated. You are what you have come to be. No more and no less. And you have made this person yourself.

The second component of this feeling is the vague realization that life, your life, is temporal—that it *will* end. It is essentially a confrontation with the certainty that someday you will cease to be. But it is not just the conceptual realization that you will die that provokes the fear and even panic that some of us feel at these times. No, it is the inability to accept this as a future event with no relevance for life to be lived until the event. In short, we discover that we cannot die! As Feifel, a psychologist who has studied the psychological problems in death and dying, puts it, "And it is in this same encounter with death that each of us discovers his hunger for immortality." To live fully and freely, we must concede our own demise and renounce immortality.

Now those who believe in some theological concept of immortality need not be offended by these words. Because it is not the notion of spiritual immortality that must be renounced. This belief can be maintained without damage to the personality. We must abandon our essential wish for the perpetual continuation of a physical life. For this is what we will not have.

People who are unable to do this have been characterized as people who live their lives "as if"—as if life were going to begin at some point in the future—"when I get my degree," or "when Johnny gets out of the Army," or "when sister has her operation." But alas, the point in time for life to begin for these people will never come. For them there will always be another "when" and existence will be of the shallow "as if" variety. They must ever remain as shells and caricatures of people, who will breathe and exist thinking that they are really going to live "when." And while they are wandering through this imitation of life, they are forfeiting time they can never recover. Again quoting Feifel, "The price for denying death is undefined anxiety, self-alienation. To completely understand himself, man must confront death, become aware of personal death."

The third major component of this uncomfortable feeling is probably the most critical of them all. This is the realization of essential loneliness. Each of us is basically alone. Love and companionship can make the terror of loneliness bearable, but these things can't change the fact of "aloneness." Here then we must again probably offend the people who protest, "No, I'm never alone, Jesus (or Buddha, or Mohammed, and so forth) is always with me." Yet the contradictions in such persons are so evident that one can scarcely bear to reveal them. We might only mention the futility of the assumption that this existence is only preparation for "real life," which begins after we abandon this one. This is the "as if" philosophy that we have pointed out to be an empty vessel that has no essence of life. This kind of thinking also denies the fact and importance of our temporal nature. This denial then prevents the confrontation with our finiteness that is so necessary to life itself. Most of all, the pitiful and cruel predicament that is ours when we or someone we love must die is painful and permits no resolution. It can be stated crudely like this: "This life is temporary and is preparation for immortality, and this glorious immortality will surely be given to my fine father (or my infant daughter, or my good mother), who has died."

"But if I believe this, then why do I feel this way!" This paradox in feeling cannot be resolved and will be repressed (in time) to serve always as a limiting constriction on our freedom.

The fact is, as Feifel has found in his research on the meaning of death, that "religious" people (professing a belief in life after death) fear death more than do people who have no such beliefs. This contradiction in behavior, as opposed to professed belief, is a surface manifestation of the torment within.

So then the vague feeling of "disease" that we opened this chapter with is a combination of three facets of the human condition that Allport has characterized as "dreadful freedom," and which we may label as the "curse of humanness." Briefly, these factors are:

1. our unilateral responsibility for what we are, and what we are to be.
2. our finite nature *which will be coincided* by death.
3. our essential condition of loneliness.

___

Self-determination

Man has attempted in various ways through the ages to deny his personal responsibility for what he is and what he will come to be. He has put himself in the hands of the "gods." He has bewailed and bemoaned his treatment at the altar of "fate." He has accepted the assumptions of Freud, and, oddly enough, some theologians, that his future is "determined." Experiences over which he has no control have charted his course, never to be changed. Some religious sects have gone so far as to profess the belief that it's all written down in some celestial book and that man's only purpose in this life is to try to understand and accept what must be.

But another group of men concerned with this problem of humanness have an idea which is at one and the same time thrilling and terrifying. It is simple and profound—"we are what we determine we will be." Another way of saying this is that our involvement in life and our determination of our values, our beliefs, and our commitments are the sum total of what we are. Certain temporal and physical events are determined or are governed by chance, but these things are not the essence of our humanness. Only "I" can determine what the essence of my humanness is and what it is to become. And a part of this determination is my decision to be "one with mankind," to be or not to be a part of the potential humanness of all men. As John Donne puts it, "Any man's death diminishes me, because I am involved in mankind."

It is the realization and acceptance of the responsibility for what we are that provokes a part of the "feeling of dread" that constitutes what Sartre and others have called man's existential awareness. Rollo May has said that man is the "organism who makes certain values—prestige, power, tenderness, love—more important than pleasure and even more important than survival itself."

This kind of philosophy commits many in education, government, and fields of psychology to the proposition not only that man can "grow," can "become," can "develop," but that he is compelled "to become" or not, he is compelled "to grow" or to atrophy. Shakespeare's works have survived mainly because they have illustrated so vividly the essential human dilemmas, and he so aptly illustrated the most important of them all in a phrase that every schoolboy can quote, "To be, or not to be? That is the question." And every schoolboy knows at some level of awareness that this phrase is important, but he probably doesn't yet know why.

We've talked about man's need to confront the fact of his

personal death. But one more word about it. This confrontation is an essential part of man's answer to the question of
"being" discussed above. He must find some meaningful
personal resolution of the fact of personal finiteness before
he is free to consider what he will be and what he will
become. This compelling confrontation is not easy; it is not
pleasant; it is not without its terror, but it is necessary, and
if met successfully, it will be a measure of strength.

"The loss of illusions and the discovery of identity,
though painful at first, can be ultimately exhilarating and
strengthening," says A. Maslow, a psychologist who has
helped others through their confrontation with humanness.
For those who maintain that man is a deterministic pawn,
Maslow goes on to say, "The Americans have learned that
political democracy and economic prosperity do not in
themselves solve any of the basic value problems. There is
no place else to turn but inward, to the self, as the locus of
values."

I wish to remind those who hold no brief for an "encounter with others," or for an "involvement in mankind," that
man does not live by bread alone, but without bread he does
not live. Hungry, cold, oppressed, and cruelly treated people
have no time to consider what they are to be. We who fail
to help them have determined this for them; the essence of
this determination is that they will not become human.

The third "agony," then, of the human condition is
loneliness. Through our struggle with the other two primary
conditions—self-determination and temporality—we discover the fact of our aloneness. The clear realization of what
aloneness really is probably is the most terrifying of all our
burdens. It is certainly the most difficult to think about and
to finally come to terms with. Death and self-determination
fade in their terror beside the certainty of our knowledge
that we are alone. C. P. Snow says, "Each of us is alone."

The shallow man will never confront the human agonies of self-awareness, temporality, and loneliness. And he will never suffer the greatest pains, but he will never feel the sublime joys. Man's emotional existence (which is the important part of life) is apparently one of certain behavioral reciprocals. Seemingly one cannot experience great delight without having also experienced great pain. We probably don't need to demonstrate this clinically or in the lab. We need only to look around us. Who are the loving ones? Who are those persons that "touch" us? Who are the compassionate ones? Almost always they are those who have met life with vitality and with a realization that the encounter is real and is theirs to confront or ignore, and these people have met pain, disappointment, death, rejection, fear, and despair. But from these encounters they have gained the reciprocal capacity to know joy, love, compassion, and human fulfillment.

The most pitiful and awful of the fates of man is the possibility of going through life without struggling, painfully but joyfully, with the tasks of humanness which confront each of us. The consequence of our failure to make this confrontation is a personal, empty shallowness that will condemn us to count out our hours and days "in quiet desperation."

Touch me not

"First things first" is a folk adage known by most of us. The validity of the adage has been demonstrated in each of our lives. It's just a convenient way of observing that we must tend to the basic requirements of any undertaking before we can go on to the other responsibilities of the task. Our task of personal emotional development is really no different. We have to take care of the primary needs before we are free to elaborate our personalities into reasonable semblances of maturity.

Unfortunately, if these basic needs were never adequately met, we may spend the rest of our lives in mostly inappropriate attempts to satisfy them. I suggest "inappropriate attempts" because the actions designed to satisfy the security and comfort needs of the five-year-old look awkward, uncomfortable, and unappealing when we see them manifested almost unchanged in the thirty-year-old. But we can't escape these demands. They will be satisfied or they will serve as disguised motives for most of our actions in later life, serving to subvert productive behavior and personality growth.

Psychologists speak of basic needs or primary reinforcers, using that term in its technical sense. The primary reinforcers or needs for all humans are limited to just a few things in our universe. For survival we need food, water, air, and shelter. There are no other basic needs. That's all the infant is born with as instinctive requirements for life. Of course, in the process of supplying these needs, somebody handles the baby, gives him his food and water, and makes sure that his "shelter" is warm and dry. In a most primary fashion, this caring behavior comes to be equated with the supplying of life's basic needs. It is a "hand" that gives food and water, and a "face" and "voice" that accompany the act. Hands and arms and soft breasts protect and repair and soothe the ravages to the baby's shelter, which is his body. Air and the accompanying breathing process seldom assume much value as a reinforcing agent because they are automatically available and are seldom, or never, associated with a "giving" person.

Then life's basic needs come to be associated with acts performed by a person or persons. The satisfactions or dissatisfactions of these needs soon become equivalent to our feelings and relationships with first our caretakers, and then our close associates and friends. In a real sense then, other people supply or deny our symbolic needs for basic life satisfactions. This is why gratification and punishment from those we depend on for sustenance (or their substitutes in later life, such as teachers, bosses, and spouses) can be so rewarding and growth engendering, or so threatening and inhibiting.

If you really feel that this formulation of how we carry infantile needs into our adult life is far-fetched, observe the importance, feeling, and ceremony that surround the acts of eating and drinking as a social custom. Smoking as a directly oral symbolic equivalent of getting basic sustenance is the proof par excellence of this.

One physical behavior accompanying the supplying of basic needs from the first instance is touching. In the beginning, none of the life-sustaining behaviors can be accomplished without touching. This essential touching is usually elaborated into hugging, kissing, rocking, fondling, caressing, and other physical acts that culminate in close and prolonged bodily contact. Then touching comes to be an elaboration of and equivalent to the provision of food, water, and bodily comfort. In fact, for most of us, touching serves as the most direct reinforcing behavior in our lives, and of course usually the act of touching is accompanied by feelings. Sometimes this touching is received with warmth and pleasure, but often it is repulsed and despised in a manifestation of the most primary rejection of human interaction.

The ways we are touched

I did not want to be touched. I shuddered inwardly when a friend put an arm on my shoulder or when a relative hugged and kissed me on meeting. I assiduously avoided the friend who persisted in holding my arm or putting his hand on my shoulder when he talked to me. I didn't like to be jammed tightly into a car when I would be forced to sit in contact with someone else. My family and friends must have seen me duck the usual hugs and kisses attendant on arriving and departing from the group. I really could not abide close physical contact with my wife or children. A few seconds of hugging and I simply had to escape! I felt trapped, strangled, frantic, and hostile if the contact wasn't terminated in a short time. Even now, I find it difficult to linger when saying good-bye, because protracted departures are really symbolically prolonged bodily contacts. In short, I could not accept even symbolic sustenance in the form of physical contact from my friends and family. I coldly and harshly discouraged anyone from approaching and contacting me. If they persisted, I got out of their way or turned chilly enough in my behavior to cause them to back away to a "safer" distance. This phenomenon is not such a strange or unusual one. All of us know people who obviously are uncomfortable if anybody touches them. They evade any situation when touching is likely to occur and usually such bodily shy people are also emotionally shy. They (and probably me) are cold, aloof, and uninvolved people. They are often characterized as cool and collected in an emergency situation. In fact, such people are usually seething emotionally and their calmness is the mask they develop to hide their intense efforts at mastering and controlling people and events around them so they won't be touched.

A coming and a going

The days working at the Children's Center grew to be more routine and comfortable for me, if not more exciting.

A usual day found me evaluating one child on the intake unit at the hospital, and one resident child on one of the wards. I hated it when I had to see one of the kids in the custodial cottages. These children were profoundly retarded, and most of them were severely brain damaged. Many had assorted crippling conditions. In spite of good care, these cottages smelled of urine, vomit, and feces, plus the peculiar body odor that is often exuded by severely retarded, disturbed, or ill people.

I'd examine my two children, write my reports, and that was my day. Sometimes it was a stressful job, although it was also often boring. I wanted to do something else, learn something more. My supervisor agreed to my request for some new work, and she assigned me to develop a counseling group for five mildly retarded teenage boys who were discipline problems. In addition, I started therapy sessions with two autistic children. One of these was a boy about four years old. He was named Tommy. The other was a pretty little girl of five named Tina.

Tommy and Tina were my real challenges. They were severely autistic, had no usable speech, and were grossly hyperactive. Any kind of relationship was highly threatening to them. My therapy efforts consisted almost entirely of trying to make contact with them. Both of them regarded me as an object, not as a person. They would try to move me out of their way as I would move a chair if it was in my path. They would never make eye contact, and they would not even react to any verbal efforts at communication on my part. My attempts to make physical contact would cause them to react with intense anxiety. If I managed to corner one of them, they would respond with rage until they managed to break free.

A year of twice weekly sessions with my boys' group and individual sessions three times a week with Tommy and

Tina was therapeutically instructive, but frustrating. I don't think anybody "got better." But I learned a great deal. After a year, Tommy would come to me to get a piece of gum; he would hold my hand briefly for his reward. Tina learned that she could get to play in the sandbox, a great treat for her, if she made eye contact with me and tried to speak. I finally taught her to say her name. Slow therapeutic progress for a year's work!

My boys didn't even make that much progress. At least I didn't think they did. Every session was chaotic—survival of the fittest. Imagine my surprise when two of the house mothers at the boys' cottages told me, "You are really doing wonders for those boys." To my amazement, they reported that the boys were making better adjustments in their "homes" and seemed to be happier and easier to get along with.

I know that I learned at least one important lesson in my efforts to help these children. I found that the first task of any therapy procedure is to make meaningful contact with my client, and I found that this was excruciatingly difficult. People don't like to be touched when they are hurting. They resist being touched both physically and emotionally. It's ironic, but fitting, that I could not see that I resisted being touched as vigorously as did those suffering kids.

At the end of my first year at the Children's Center, I was offered a job as a psychologist in an agency serving exceptional children in another state. The responsibilities of this new job were similar to my work at the Children's Center. However, now I was working with children in the public schools and I was traveling all over the state. After our move to a new home, I called the therapist recommended by the hospital and began a new attempt to find myself with him.

Dr. Carl T. was a psychiatrist in private practice doing therapy with individuals and with groups, and he agreed to take me on. Dr. T. was about forty-five, a trifle pudgy, and graying a bit. I found him to be kind, patient, and comfortable. But I treated him as formally as I would the envoy from a foreign country.

After a year of weekly sessions, I still reacted to his overtures of friendship with suspicion and polite correctness. Occasionally his patience eroded under this treatment.

"Damn," he exclaimed one day. "I've called you Russell for six months now. Why do you still call me Dr. T.?"

After a year of therapy, I still had not been "touched." It never occurred to me that to be physically touched by anyone was important, and I had not really been even emotionally touched. My relationship with my therapist remained cognitive and intellectual, and we focused on my life outside the therapy hours. In a word, our relationship was sterile, and it remained that way because we had not made contact in any real sense. In retrospect, I can see that Carl pushed in the direction of personalizing our relationship. He tried to give me the opportunity to contact him. He offered personal friendship and confidence, and he proved over and over that he would be open to overtures from me. I resisted. I insisted that he was my doctor, and I was his patient. After all, we were two adults trying to attend to a problem, weren't we? Now I know that we were an adult and a child trying to meet the needs of a thirty-five-year-old infant.

And I insisted that we deal with my difficulties in an objective, scientific way. After all, it was simply a matter of uncovering unconscious resistances, feelings, and memories, wasn't it? That's what Freud said anyhow. In reality, it was necessary to make conscious certain aspects of the unconscious, namely my intense need to be cared for and nurtured. Finally one day we did that.

Our therapy hours had become dry and dull. I guess they really always were. There was the formal recitation from me on the events of my week, a new description (after hundreds of times I was hard pushed) of my suffering and depression; a renewed plea from me to be "fixed" so I could stop suffering, and another response from Carl that I could begin to live if I would quit doing what I was doing. This frustrated the hell out of me.

"How can I quit what I'm doing?" I would shout. "Tell me how dammit, tell me." I had to find it for myself.

The weeks faded into months, and we came together time after time in a grindingly dull and dry repetition of all our previous meetings. It was like a stylized dance of the puppets or the ten-thousandth recitation of a poem—same dialogue, same response, same feelings, same outcome.

My frustration grew and I'm sure that Carl's did too. I knew I simply wasn't doing anything. I wasn't getting anywhere. I knew it, but I didn't know why. Finally my own intense feelings of inertia and failure got to be more overwhelming than my need to keep things the same.

On that day I approached our session with feelings of anxiety and agitation. I knew I had to do something, but I didn't know what. I felt deeply that I had to do something to get myself moving, to quit repeating the failure of our relationship over and over.

At last the door opened. Carl stuck his head out and smiled, "Come in."

We sat there awhile, with me saying nothing and him replying with an alert but gentle silence. The minutes dragged by. More silence. My anxiety grew. I was almost literally shaking.

"I'm afraid," I murmured. Carl replied, "I can see that." "My hands are shaking" I held out one trembling hand for him to see. He looked, but said nothing.

"Goddamn," I exploded. "Aren't you going to do or say something?"

In a nondefensive tone he replied, "What is it you want me to do or say?"

And then from my lips I was surprised to hear, "I want you to hold my hand." I couldn't believe I had said it! A thirty-five-year-old man asking another man to hold his hand, like a child or a homosexual. I decided that it was a child who said that.

"All right," Carl replied. He moved his chair nearer mine and took my hand in his. My anxiety grew to unbearable limits and after a few seconds I had to release my clasp and take my hand back. But it was a first for me. I had surrendered my anonymous objectivity, and I had permitted a relationship to develop which depended on the gratification of my primary needs to sustain it.

"I wondered how long it would take you to do something like that," Carl smiled. "I almost gave up the hope that you ever could."

"I really didn't know what you meant when you talked about resisting you and maintaining distance until now. I didn't know what you were talking about when you said I had to give up to win. Finally, I understand," I said. And I did. I guess Professor Freud must have known something after all!

Hurting

These moments reduced the sharp edge of my torment. But it wasn't enough. I was still hurting, still hoping, still tormented. Emotional pain is real. It pierces and penetrates the secret, hidden places in your body and soul. It grinds, thrusts, wrenches, and rips into the fiber of your being.

It is pain. Pain of a kind and degree that is difficult to describe to you. I have felt many times as if all the demons of hell were tearing at my mind and body. It has hurt so much that I have writhed in agony and wept tears of despair. The agony is excruciating, sharp, and acute. One longs for unconsciousness (or mental dissociation) to escape it. Perhaps some have found a way. One is forced to make an attempt to understand why he hurts so. Probably that's why one sufferer thinks he's being poisoned. At least that rationally accounts for such pain, whether it's true or not. Another "knows" that his brain is under the noxious influence of radio waves from Mars. Some people abandon this attempt at logic and "shut down" that part of their minds and use only a small, circumscribed section that is relatively free from pain. Then the person who has that crippled mind simply sits all day in one position and stares into space. Or perhaps he draws boxes or wheels on a piece of paper some kind attendant at the hospital gives him.

The shut-down part of that person's mind probably decays or atrophies from isolation and disuse. After an indeterminate period of time (governed by what forces we don't know), a few years, or sometimes only a few weeks, this part of the mind is the sole province of the "demons" and their isolation in a divided mind serves to reduce the pain they cause. But by their isolation, they become firmly entrenched and likely can never be displaced.

Then there are a sizeable number of those, myself included, who apparently are unable to give up part of their minds in exchange for a lessening of pain. If I could make the swap, I probably would. But they and I are forced to struggle on and on. Sometimes I get a glimpse of what it means emotionally to be "free." What a wonderful, magnificent feeling. Not only is the pain gone, but you feel able to cope with things, to give of yourself, to be interested and concerned about others, to look at the world and see promise rather than despair. Too bad, but those moments are far too few. Most of the time, you are engrossed in an inner battle for control. Unfortunately, the adversary has many advantages. He has several points of attack—the intellect, the emotions, the body. If one of these doesn't yield, then the attacks shift to one of the other fronts. At times, and these times are the worst, noxious advances are made on all fronts.

The pounding sick headache, the spasmodic, cramping gut, the debilitating diarrhea, dizziness, clumsiness, tics, and paralyzed muscles. These are only a small sample of the attacks that can be mounted on the body front alone.

The real versatility of your opponent is shown in the confrontation with your emotions and your intellect. The range of pathology possible in these human spheres is almost indescribable and the signs and symptoms uncountable. But some bright people try to describe them and to count them. And they probably do a respectable job. But they omit the essence of the pain in their description. They may say, for instance, "Delusions are common in this syndrome." They should say, "Delusions are common in this syndrome, resulting from the sufferer's attempts to make some sense out of the exquisite agony he is experiencing."

Man is compelled by his very nature, which is still the human condition, no matter how deranged, to try in every way possible to make his experience logical. So his mind invents a "cover story" which explains the events he is experiencing. You have to do something when your body, your feelings, and your judgment are in utter chaos and turmoil. You cannot sit on the sidelines and observe. You do what you can because you must do something.

The ways out

Then one struggles over the years. Days and weeks and even months become too small to count as units of time. You see some rays of light, but you feel far too many stabs of despair. Like a fish on a line, you wriggle and squirm to escape. If a good portion of your mind is unaffected, you see the "sick" part of your mind with some clarity. And this is frightening, because one sees in one's mind the black pit of terror, the confused tangle of malfunctioning logic, the engulfing morass of despair and hopelessness. After you see these things with some degree of vividness (in a panic state or perhaps an acute agitation or maybe in a hallucination), you must take some action. Seeking help is one of those actions: from your family physician, or minister, or some trusted friend or relative. Unfortunately, you feel like a fool when you try to tell them how much it hurts. It is a bit silly, isn't it? Not logical in the least. Certainly not mature. So they react as you virtually force them to—with kindness and reassurance or with suggestions for some emotional dodge that helps you stave off the "sickness" for a little while longer.

Sometimes you can't bring yourself to seek comfort and help and sometimes you haven't had a clear look at the disturbed part of your mind. Then you may get drunk or take drugs, beat your wife, spend all your money in a mad frenzy, or wriggle about in other ways to escape the pain. Of course, the most prevalent way to stop it is to extinguish the host, to destroy one's body.

However, this method has one major disadvantage. It is not reversible or correctable. Many people every day try it anyhow. Suicide is currently the tenth leading cause of death. For those who try it, the point and degree of suffering have overbalanced the point and degree of comfort, and they make the choice that ceasing to live is preferable to living in pain. Many, many people who struggle with symptoms of depression and anxiety reach the time when they recognize only two choices—to live miserably or to die quickly.

If there were a physical disease that manifested itself in some particularly ugly way, such as pustulating sores or a sloughing off of the flesh accompanied by pain of an intense and chronic nature, readily visible to everyone, and if that disease affected fifteen million people in our country, and further, if there were virtually no help or succor for most of these persons, and they were forced to walk among us in their obvious agony, we would rise up as one social body in sympathy and in anger. We would give of our resources, both human and economic, and we would plead and demand that this suffering be eased. There isn't such a physical disease, but there is such a disease of the mind, and about fifteen million people around us are suffering from it. But we have not risen in anger and sympathy, although they are walking among us and crying in their pain and anguish.

Their cry takes many forms. Some few kill their fellows. Some abuse, emotionally and physically, those they love; some write petitions of hate and wear costumes of evil; some lay down their bodies and simply expire; others hasten the process with a gun or knife; some cries take the form of the drunk or the junkie or the pervert. These are the more dramatic, demanding cries that society has to answer in some fashion. However, most of the cries are far less dramatic or interesting. They manifest themselves in the drawn face, in a timid, hesitant manner. They show themselves as poor work, as uncooperativeness, as quarreling or irritability. On a broader social scale, these cries take the form of civil disobedience, riots, and wars.

For the most part, the cries are unheeded. So one body with its troubled mind refuses eternally to relate to the rest of the world; another turns on the gas and waits impatiently for release. Some wind up with their bodies humanely mutilated by various surgeons. Still another seeks some comfort from liquor or morphine or LSD. The occasional one kills or assaults or rapes. But the answer to their various and desperate cries is all too inadequate. "Be still," we say; "be mature," we exhort; "behave," we shout; "be independent," we moralize; "snap out of it," we advise; "you'd better watch your step," we warn. To characterize these answers, and those of like value, as inadequate is an almost ludicrous understatement of their worthlessness.

How long?

I thought I would wait until it was all over. That seems to be the customary thing when one is trying to write about a tragedy or hardship. That sounds rather dramatic, doesn't it? I guess it has to be dramatic. We usually struggle to live when death seems to be the preferred alternative.

So I've waited for over six years, and it's not over yet. If I'm going to write something that may mean something to other people, I'd better begin. I must confess that I'm writing these words with a "let me tell you about my operation" attitude. I need to say some things, call it therapy if you choose. Some of you who read these words are searching just as desperately as I.

The trouble with writing about a disturbed, sick mind and soul is that in general it is uninteresting and seldom filled with action or uniqueness. Depression must be the most undynamic and uninteresting phenomenon in the world. Almost by definition, it suggests the abandonment of interest. Some of you know this. I would like to tell others, since depression is of critical concern to the person who suffers it. It is my aim to try to tell you something about the inner world of a person struggling with depression and anxiety. When we make the plea that words can't describe it, we are begging the question. We have to try with words.

My reading and experience in the world of the mentally ill have left me with considerable frustration. For example, a behavioral description of an acute depression may read like this: "The patient may cry readily and at great length. He may profess that he is worthless, of no utter use to the world. He may believe that he has caused natural calamities, such as floods and earthquakes. Chances are his sleep pattern is erratic with early waking the rule. He may be unable to eat at times, almost to the point of total fasting. Often he complains of various bodily dysfunctions. Headaches, nausea, abdominal pain, lower back discomfort, poor appetite, and general malaise are the most frequent complaints."

The observant reader will note that this description says not a word about the feelings of the sufferer. Most of them don't. Little is said about the vicious, unrelenting pain, pain so terrible and so inescapable that eventually the possibility of ending the suffering by death is seriously considered.

I expect that suicide is of utmost concern to the whole gamut of "mental health professionals." They are justified in their contention that they can treat only the living. The dead have abandoned any chance, however slim, of recovery. But little apparent attention is given to why self-inflicted death is so frequent in the various mental disorders. This outcome is not a natural consequence of depression, anxiety, or any other noxious emotion.

One only has to observe the feelings of someone who has recently lost a loved one to see this. Freud postulated a death wish. Others have suggested that man is endowed with "a drive to destruction." Many social scientists extend this theorizing to the broader social structure to explain war and other civil discord. Such explanations are dogmatic in nature and gratuitous in contribution. Which is to say that they offer nothing to the understanding of human nature.

One explanation of this phenomenon is so simple, so free

of psychological or psychiatric gyrations that it undoubtedly will be received coolly. In my judgment, death is chosen because suffering is so acute, so agonizing, so intolerable that a time comes, depending on the individual tolerance to pain and the support available, when *ceasing to suffer* is the most important thing in the world. Consequently, we have self-inflicted physical death and many of its small imitators, some more vicious than that which the victim would escape. I refer specifically to such outcomes as crimes of violence (not all due to mental illness by any means), drug addiction, psychotic states, and alcoholism.

What determines which alternative the individual will "select" in an attempt to escape something that he can no longer bear? I'm not sure that he really has much choice in the matter. It may well be that constitutional factors are important. Apparently some people are born more constitutionally able to tolerate pain than others.

Undoubtedly, lifestyle plays an important part. How has the person escaped the nonpathological pain in the past? Has he used aggressive physical or verbal action, resorted to fantasy and daydreaming, shifted the burden to someone else, and on and on through the almost unlimited repertoire of human behavior. The mechanism that is finally resorted to is probably a culmination and a combination of heredity, lifestyle, present circumstances, and self-determination. Self-determination, you say? Yes. Ultimately, even the person who kills himself physically must choose his weapon. So we do have some measure of choice. And it is to this even so slight indication of man's "freedom" that I look for hope.

Hope

The hope that we look for is the hope generated by acceptance and empathy. The hope that is reflected in the response "tell me about it" or "you must be very frightened" or "I know it hurts." Most people in distress come to someone else for understanding, acceptance, and compassion. They don't expect solutions or advice, and they certainly don't need criticism. But what do we do when someone comes to us in pain? What do we say when a friend tells us that his life is misery or that he's unhappy or he can't sleep or he's worried about his job, his wife, or his children?

Think about the response you might make if your best friend came to you and said he was afraid his boss was displeased with him and he might lose his job. What would be your first comments? If you're like most of us, you would offer reassurance. "Look, he gave you a raise last year; he wouldn't do that if he thought your work was unsatisfactory. Besides, he's never told you that you weren't doing well." Your friend sighs; he can see that you didn't hear the message he gave you: "I'm afraid."

At another level, we might even tell him, "Don't worry, things will work out" or "Half the things you worry about never come true." Perhaps we really turn him off by offering advice. "You should work harder. Put in some overtime; that'll really impress him."

How much better and how much more helpful we could be to each other if we could respond to the emotional message of pleas for help. Why can't we say to our friend, "I can see you are really worried; tell me about it." Think what this kind of response can lead to for him. He can explore his worry. He can verbalize it and put it in perspective. He can listen to himself and see how it really sounds when described to someone else. He is freed to think about himself and his feelings openly rather than defending his beliefs and ideas to a skeptical listener. Why don't we answer cries for help this way? Why do we persist in questioning, probing, denying, rationalizing, and reassuring? Probably because we are afraid ourselves. His fear makes us afraid. His doubts make us uncertain. His anxiety makes us tremble.

Yet, it's a paradox that open exploration of fear, frustration, and anxiety serves to reduce those feelings. Denial and unrealistic reassurance serve to increase them. These intensified, unrelieved, and unexpressed feelings drain our energy and sap our emotional resources. They corrupt our pleasure in living and our joy in others. They bind us to a rigid, unfulfilling, and unproductive way of using ourselves and of relating to others.

In the pages that follow, I'll try to describe my own struggles to contain and overcome my fears and frustrations, my hostile rages and unrequited needs. I'm not unique in experiencing these emotions. All of us are subject to their influences in our lives. My great psychological mistake was that I denied my feelings as long as I could, and I finally refused to share them with others when I could no longer deny them.

My attempts to put myself back together after my collapse were not always successful. Like the proverbial "sinner," I was subject to frequent backsliding. I think, though, that I learned something each time I pulled myself through another self-induced crisis. This kind of experience and this kind of learning contributed a great deal to my subsequent development as a psychologist, even if it taught me nothing more than to be sensitive to how I had failed a client.

It must be human nature. Whatever that is! So many of us operate our lives with the apparent conviction that "if I don't talk about it, it won't happen," or "if I don't think about it, it won't be true." That's how I behaved, and sometimes still do. And that's how many unhappy people manipulate their own lives and the lives of those they have in their care and keeping.

After I had experienced my own psychic disintegration,

which I'll describe more completely in the next few chapters, and after I had completed my training and got myself back together, I began practice as a psychologist seeing children in distress. One of the children I saw, a little girl named Sue, was required to repress, ignore, and deny her feelings. Her mother brought her to me because of frequent, repeated, and terrifying nightmares.

Sue was withdrawn and sullen, and, at five years of age, she had no friends, and she had no fun. In her history was a long series of hospitalizations for ear and throat infections. She continued to have a chronic ear problem which was going to require more medical treatment.

"Was Sue very upset over her trips to the hospital and the operations?" I asked her mother. "Oh, no," her mother replied proudly, "she never cried or complained one time. In fact, she never cries."

I thought to myself, "I'll bet she didn't! You just didn't hear her."

In play sessions with Sue, after we got to know each other, I brought in a toy table, a bed, and doll figures of a man, a woman, and a child. I put the child doll in the bed and put the woman beside the bed.

"The baby's sick," I said to Sue, "and here's mamma. What happens now?"

At first Sue wouldn't play at all. "I don't know," she insisted stubbornly. "Well," I said, "we've got to do something; the baby's sick." I waited longer than Sue could stand. Finally she spoke for the mother doll, "Come on, we've got to go to the doctor and get some medicine."

I inquired, "What does the baby say?"

"Nothing," Sue replied stubbornly.

With that, she picked up the baby and the mother and "took" them to the doctor.

"Let me tell a story now, Sue." I took the baby doll and put her back in the bed with the mother alongside.

Now I spoke for the dolls. "Baby, your ears are infected again. We're going to have to go to the doctor and get some medicine." Baby replied, "But, I'm afraid. It'll hurt me."

I looked at Sue, who was absorbedly following the action. "What does mamma say now, Sue?" I asked. Almost automatically she replied, "You're a big girl now. Big girls don't cry. The doctor won't hurt you."

We paused for a moment, still looking at the dolls and thinking about what was happening. I spoke for the baby, "I'm afraid. He'll hurt me. I'm gonna cry." I sobbed a few times for the baby. Then I picked her up and gave her to the mamma. Then the mamma said, "I know you're afraid, and I'll be with you all the time, and if it hurts, I'll hold your hand, and I won't let go."

Sue sat quietly watching. Two big tears filled her eyes and ran down her cheeks. Her mother said she never cried.

On psychotherapy

6

My EXPERIENCE indicates that the business called psychotherapy (or analysis or counseling or any other name used to describe the so-called talking therapies) is a system of contradictions.

It is rewarding—It is a waste of time and money
It is fulfilling—It is meaningless
It relieves pain—It induces agony
It is easy—It's the hardest of hard work
It heals—It has no effect

Psychotherapy is all of these and more. If you are involved in it long enough, all of these things will be true at some time or other. I went into therapy because I really had no choice. My personal distress was so intolerable that I had to seek help somewhere, anywhere. No doubt it is easy for some people. For me, it was difficult. I think the problem I am experiencing in trying to write about it reflects this.

Have you ever tried to talk with someone for forty-five minutes (inflation has shrunk the "fifty-minute hour") when the topic is yourself? It's not so bad for the first twenty or thirty sessions. You can cover your life history, childish and adult escapades, hopes and fears, sins and guilts, triumphs and tragedies, but after awhile you run dry. Your history is exhausted. Then you turn to something a little closer to yourself—current events and feelings—what I felt, what I said, what he said, how she looked, why I felt that way, how I felt. This task would seemingly supply an inexhaustible source of material to carry you through each hour. But, alas, you begin to repeat yourself, and you know it. And you know he knows that you know it. How many ways can you describe your depression and despair? How many times can you illustrate your anxiety and dread? Finally you really run dry. So far you have spent anywhere from about $500, if you either aren't too bright, or aren't too sick, up to about $5,000 if you are unlucky enough to be bright and sick and reasonably rich.

Then what do you do? For one thing, you hate the SOB who has taken so much of your money, time, and energy, implied he would help, and has done nothing of any value. You still hurt, can't sleep, face agonizing periods of despair, think about ending it all. And he has sat there calmly and just listened. At least you think he has listened! Undoubtedly there are times when he didn't even do that.

So now you spend several therapy periods seeking vengeance. If you're the lucky, open type, you tell him he's a money-stealing, incompetent charlatan. If, however, your approach lies in the other more subtle directions, and you can't tolerate the thought that you do hate him, and justifiably—he hasn't helped—then you tell him what a fine, helpful, understanding man he is. And you tell him and tell him and tell him. Hoping, I suppose, that he will get the implied message and begin acting like a fine, helpful person!

Then too, you may be the kind of person who can't strike back at all. You may simply become depressed. You have been failed again. You can despise yourself, but you can't hate those who have failed you. Somehow you have learned that you must not. After all, who can really fail you except those who matter to you? A stranger? A casual friend? A professional colleague? No, the only one who is really in a position to fail you is someone you love. But your anger is there. It's got to be. You haven't been helped, and you dare not love anyone. So whom can you hate? Your old, trusty self, that's who. That's who has been punished all your life when you were failed, or thought you were failed, by someone you love, which psychologically is the same thing.

So you reach an impass. This is a dangerous phase of time in treatment. If you are so inclined, you can say the hell with it and quit. Don't chastise yourself that you have failed. Your therapist is the one who has failed. Of course, you will do the further suffering, not he. But you can stew in the satisfaction of your right to suffer.

Then if you can't quit, you can adopt him as your long lost father (or mother or lover), and try to get him to protect you forever. Just as you tried, and failed, with your real father or mother or lover. Or you can destroy yourself with a cataclysmic depressive anxiety episode and go back to a hospital or back to the psychological "womb." Or you can really do it up brown and accomplish your two major goals, revenge and relief of pain. You can kill yourself. That is really a pretty effective method. Your therapist will suffer (although he will eventually repress or rationalize the experience), and you stop the pain. The only disadvantage to this alternative is all too obvious. You won't be around to enjoy either his suffering or your own relief.

The turning point

This is the point in your relationship with your therapist when the successful therapists are separated from the failures. Notice, I didn't say the patient fails or succeeds. The therapist must stand steadfast and calm against your assaults. If he "runs scared," you may stay in treatment, but he has essentially failed with you.

In my initial try at therapy, I reached this point after six months. I was a slow learner! I remember that one day in my misery I said, with apparent conviction, "I feel like I could explode." This must have frightened my therapist. He drew back in his chair and said rather hastily, "Well, don't do it here." It was all over then. I continued to see him for about a year after that. But I was just marking time. He lost me at that moment.

Not only must your therapist stand his ground, he also must help you to stay out of a depression or an anxiety state and out of a hospital, and to remain alive and remain in treatment. This is a large order and many so-called therapists, both medical and nonmedical, can't do it. Of course, they fool themselves and their clients that they are effective, since many people get well in spite of their therapists' treatment. Or they can settle for the small gain they have achieved if they aren't in too much distress.

How can he keep you and help you avoid either physical or psychological disaster? For one thing, as we said, he stands fast. You can see that someone you depend on has strength and stability. You are compelled to note that he won't cooperate in your self-destruction and that he won't retaliate in kind to your hostility. If he is defensive or petulant or anxious and afraid, this is the time that you will find him out. And you will have been failed again.

Then he must stand fast. But he must also show an unconditional regard and acceptance, not of what you do or feel or think or say, but of you. This is another way of saying that he must like you. And I use "like" in its common meaning. If he doesn't really feel this way, he can't fake it. He will be tested many times in many ways.

The one other thing that he must do is make himself available to you, both physically and emotionally. By physically available I mean that he sees you when and where you need him. He may be tested on this. It's at this stage that some therapists "cop out." They rationalize and give logical, compelling theoretical reasons why they never see a patient outside of regular scheduled visits, or why they have an unlisted telephone that you can't call. Perhaps they should review their policies on this issue. It could be that they are defending their inability to deal effectively with you in a crisis or that they are just plain lazy. If they are inclined to the soft life, they shouldn't have chosen psychotherapy as a career. Along with his physical presence, the therapist must bring his emotional self. He "shows" that he does care, that he is concerned about your distress, that he will not abandon you, literally or figuratively.

Then if he does these things, if he stands fast, gives unconditional acceptance and makes himself available to you, he should keep you. But sadly, he sometimes doesn't. Some people are too disturbed, too overwhelmed by a body or a mind that can't tolerate the pain, and they are sometimes lost. Sometimes they are lost for good—to a hospital, to the bottle or to drugs, to prison, to death, or perhaps simply to a life of "quiet desperation." Even if this battle is lost, you may still come back for a new try, and often at another time and another place with another person, you can make it; you can win the war. Your way has been helped by all that you and he have done before, all that you don't have to do again.

Winning and losing

Successful psychotherapy is somewhat like winning a lottery. If it happens to you, it's wonderful. But relying on psychotherapy to relieve the suffering of all emotionally disturbed people is like depending on a lottery to solve the financial problems of all poor people. There just isn't enough to go around and moreover, some people can't tolerate that kind of help. It comes too late; it's too time and money consuming; and its effectiveness is often destroyed by capricious circumstances beyond control like deaths, illnesses, moves, and job changes. In addition, it seems to me that psychotherapy is not often appropriate for those who are out of step with the marching forces of social movement itself.

I must admit that I'm not certain what my years in treatment have done for me. I don't know if I have been helped or not. I made the observation one day to my therapist that I wasn't certain if "this" had any effect on my "illness." But that I did feel I was a better person because of it. Maybe I was just as depressed and anxious, yet somehow I was better. I can't seem to describe this feeling well. Perhaps it's because I simply want to believe that all those hours haven't been in vain. I almost must believe that.

The effectiveness or lack of effectiveness of psychotherapy provokes raging controversy in the fields of psychology and psychiatry. The most objective observers seem to agree that there is some evidence that "it" is effective to some degree. There seems to be little conclusive evidence, however, on how effective it is, and what kinds of people with what kinds of trouble are helped most by it. There is no doubt about it, psychotherapy as a method of treating mental disorders is extremely limited. For instance, the "best" patient for psychotherapy is relatively young, fairly intelligent, well motivated, comes from a middle-class background, and is not too disturbed. In short, he is not the "sickest" or the hardest to treat of the emotionally ill.

All experts agree that psychotherapy is successful only for those people who are well motivated.* Yet, it is exactly this sphere of emotional functioning, motivation, that is seriously affected by the disorder itself! The paradox is evident. Disorders of motivation are numerous and serious. Yet the major treatment modality, psychotherapy, requires good motivation in the potential client.

I'll never forget the psychiatrist who told me when we were discussing a particular woman alcoholic that he was going to have to discharge her from his care. "Why?" I asked. "Well," he says, "she won't quit drinking."

Other limitations are rather obvious. Therapy may be lengthy. It is probably going to be quite costly, and it is not generally available to many who need it. Perhaps there is no other way to deal with this most common human predicament since we grow so slowly, and our personalities and characters are shaped so subtly and so gradually that any major change in these is laboriously difficult. Yet this reasoning offers little or no consolation to the sufferer of mental anguish.

---

*There are now exceptions to this general statement, especially from the conditioning or behavioral therapists. Behaviorists have been praised and maligned. The aversive treatment of homosexuals or of dangerous persons, as shown in the movie, *A Clockwork Orange,* has been exaggerated as to its effectiveness. Such treatment is not in general clinical use. It is still pretty much confined to the experimental lab. Other uses of conditioning, including applications in the classroom with normal children and in special programs with disturbed children, have been praised as meaningful social contributions although the treatment principles are no different from aversive treatment of criminals, homosexuals, and psychopaths.

I can't decide. On those days when I feel well, I believe that psychotherapy can offer much to those who despair. But on those days when I hurt, I am certain that it has all been a tragic waste of anguished effort. Of course, the circumstances of my own condition do not prove or disprove any treatment method or theory. But I'm not interested personally in proving anything. I only know how I feel. A philosopher, Ortega y Gasset, said, "Only his sufferings and his satisfactions instruct him concerning himself."

The final hours

My travels through the therapeutic maze have left me with a variety of impressions, feelings, and beliefs. At the hospital, I had two or three thirty-minute periods of individual therapy with a psychiatrist each week. I also participated in an hour long group therapy session weekly. Of course, the various other "therapeutic" activities such as crafts, games, and physical exercises were also available. After I left the hospital, I continued individual sessions once a week with the hospital therapist. This terminated after a year when I left for another job at the Children's Center.

After I was settled in my new job, I entered therapy with Carl. I remained in treatment with him for about four years. After that, I joined one of his therapy groups, which I'll tell you more about later. I was a member of this group for almost two years. So I'm well experienced in psychotherapy.

It's unfair to my dear friend who worked so long and hard with me to summarize those hours over a six year period in a few pages in this book. But somehow I must. I just don't want to go through all of those many, many hours of tactical and strategic maneuvering. I think he will understand.

Those hours, though, are not wasted. They are not lost motion. All of those hours are necessary for the moments when your psyche abandons its shackles, or at least is freed of some of them. Usually you won't recall the precise times or the most dramatic instances. Probably there will be many little instances when a chain fell away or a small devil quit the scene. Then over the hours and days and years, you find a new freedom. But this freedom has been bought at the price of many hours of apparent waste.

I think I could illustrate the nature of those hours with an analogy of a chess player and his game. He may sit and ponder and plan and play many possible contingencies in his imagination before he moves his chess piece. Then the movement of that chess piece represents a commitment to change analogous to "movement" in psychotherapy. The literal movement of the chess piece occupied only a small fraction of the time the game required. But those long moments of contemplation and thinking and apparent inactivity were essential to the "move."

So it is in counseling and psychotherapy. The nature of the process is evolving, developing, and changing. And this kind of process requires an inordinate amount of preparation for the moment of burgeoning. The peach tree blooms in about four or five days after budding. But it took four hundred hours of near freezing temperature during the course of a long winter to prepare for that bloom.

One time, in the last year of my therapy, I bloomed! A little anyhow. This occasion was not pleasant. To the contrary, it was most painful and difficult. And only after some length of time had passed could I look back reflectively and realize that it had been a fruitful and productive moment. A moment that culminated only after some years of seemingly wasted hours of therapy.

The day before this session, I had to go to Washington,

D.C., on a business trip. I woke up that morning feeling lousy. And I felt worse as the day went by. I caught a plane out of town about midmorning. By this time I was depressed and morose. Fortunately and unfortunately, I sat beside a friend on the way. I say unfortunately because I felt so rotten I couldn't carry on a halfway rational conversation. It was fortunate, though, because he chattered all the way, and all I had to do was to appear to be listening. Even this was hard to pull off because I could hardly even bear to look at anyone.

I went to the meeting I was to attend in Washington. I tried to take some notes and pay attention to the information I needed to get. I also tried to avoid having to meet or talk with anyone there. This was not easy because I knew a lot of the people there, and I had to use the "excuse me, I've got a headache" routine several times.

That evening I stood by the window in my hotel room looking out into nowhere really. I felt lost, desolate, and alone. I wondered if it would ever end. I felt near the edge of despair.

The next day I came back to town. As the hour approached for my session with "him," I grew increasingly nervous and apprehensive. I was agitated and fearful. I could only think, with some amazement at myself, "I want to call him every kind of a son of a bitch I can think of." But I divorced these thoughts from my emotions. I wasn't angry. At least I wasn't aware that I was. I only felt fearful and frightened of what I felt compelled to do.

We spent a little time in the beginning of the hour sparring around. I talked about my trip to Washington. I mentioned my despair and my feelings of hopelessness and helplessness. He made a couple of noncommittal remarks. Then we were silent. I'm sure my acute discomfort was visibly obvious. "Why are you so upset?" he said. I didn't say anything for awhile. Finally I croaked, "I want to call you some bad things." It sounded asinine even to me, but he looked serious. "Go ahead," he invited. I shook my head in despair, "I can't."

"Well," he said after awhile, "I'll help you." He continued, "Do you want to call me a Christ-killing kike?" My silence was confirmation. "How about a damn thief and a chiseling Jew for taking your money and not getting you well?" He paused, looking at me. But I couldn't look back. I was utterly miserable. I did want to say those things. Or at least something as vile and nasty and hurtful as I could.

"What about homosexual?" he continued relentlessly. "Do you want to call me a queer?" I still couldn't talk. Finally I said, "Yes, I did want to say those things to you and about you, but I don't know why."

"Okay," he says, in a matter of fact way. "Now they are said." He seemed to smile ever so slightly. "So, what else is new?"

And this then was a moment of blooming for me. Such a little moment. Not much was done, and it didn't take much time. I was not even able to mouth the words of hurt I wanted to say to someone I had come to like, respect, and depend on. So he had to say these things for me. He set another time for us to meet before I left for home that day. The world didn't fall in around me. And he still was my friend even though I had literally wanted to destroy him.

Although this was my time of "blooming," all was not roses thereafter. There were periods of regression, of testing, of new despair. There were, and are now, times of agony and hopelessness. There probably always will be. But this was a moment of significance. A moment of blooming that came to be only after hundreds of hours of preparation and of near freezing temperatures in my own little psychological orchard.

Loving and maturity

It's difficult for a fool to change the way he feels or thinks or acts. Every success he gets and every fortunate thing that happens to him, he attributes to his cleverness and effectiveness. On the other hand, he sees every discouragement and failure as due to the stupidity and contrariness of his friends, associates, and family. So life's events, pleasant and painful, confirm what he already believes: that he is smart and everyone else is stupid, that he is capable and others are blunderers, that he is kind and reasonable, but he is surrounded by sour malcontents. Life's experiences don't materially change him, and he usually fails to profit by what he experiences.

Surely I've learned something about myself and my life. As I examine my own mind to see what I may have learned, I discover to my rueful amazement that about all I can claim of self-discovery is to have been finally convinced that I am indeed a fool. I still sulk like a child, punish those around me for my fears and frustrations, and behave in self-destructive ways. I've learned that insight without commitment to action is a fruitless exercise in emotional masturbation. I've learned to be astounded to find that in my own life I persist in self-punishing and painful behavior, even when I recognize my own (not too subtle) efforts to rationalize my actions. "Knowing" is not necessarily the same as "doing."

To my utter disgust, I've found that my search for truth and fulfillment has led me back to the old verities and clichés that I was raised with. For instance, I really know that you do get what you give and that life returns in measurable, comparable proportions only what you are willing to put into it. You do have to "lose your life" to live it, and it turns out to be psychologically true that it is more blessed to give than to receive. I know now that life is not fair, and it doesn't have to be. All the folklore that we listened to as children and held in utter contempt now seems to have been valid.

It's as if I had struggled to the peak of the highest Tibetan mountain only to be told by the guru of wisdom at the top that the secret to life is to keep climbing. To introspect, to agonize, to go crazy, to writhe in despair, all of this in order to discover that my salvation lies in my own hands! It lies in the ability I have to refrain from acting on my destructive urges to translate my intentions into behavior, to abandon the search for the magic that will dispel fear, to grasp the opportunity to do something today that is more productive than what I did yesterday, to pull myself up slowly, and to know that it is my responsibility to do so, to suffer the "slings and arrows of outrageous fortune," and to act instead of react, to abandon my childish needs for undeserved care and succor and to eschew resentment and bitterness when I do.

My learning about myself may sound futile and barren to you. But it is great and glorious to me. I no longer am compelled to demand that all of my needs be granted by a world which really owes me nothing. I can now receive satisfaction and fulfillment by giving the succor and care that I once had to have given to me. I have learned to accept the fact that hard jobs are hard to do and that mastery of myself can only be won by tenacious effort and in small increments. I've discovered that the struggle begins again every day and that you've earned no special consideration from nature because of your accomplishments of yesterday.

I learn anew each day, because I keep forgetting it, that hate and disgust for others will cause me to suffer and that vengeance cannot be mine along with peace of mind. I've found that the offending ones are the unhappy ones and that their spite is their problem unless I make it mine. Lest I sound like "Mr. Mental Health of 1975," let me hasten to add that I digress and hate and long for magic far too often and that I must force myself to listen to my inner voice when it repeats the lessons of life to me.

Giving and getting

The transitional or pivotal point in psychological maturity occurs at the time in one's life when it becomes possible to give more than you get. This is the time of life when caring for becomes more important than being cared for. On the basis of this criterion, most of us require a long time and suffer many painful experiences before we are mature. Many of us never attain any appreciable degree of maturity; we go through life demanding care and reacting with bitterness and resentment when others cannot give it, because they themselves are seeking the same thing. Unless our needs for care are reasonably satisfied in our infancy and youth, we may never attain a satisfactory degree of adult comfort and competency. If our caring needs were seriously deprived in our early development, our seeking for succor might become so frantic, so frenzied, and so overwhelming that we actually and really are crazy.

The power and purpose of frustrated childhood rage are more awesome and lasting than most of us imagine. These remarks of a four-year-old to himself in his bath are a dramatic but accurate picture of the depth and degree of childish rage, resentment, and bitterness:

He ain't gonna do nothing.
He's just sitting there forever.
He won't eat his peas or his meat or even his cake.
He won't take candy or gum or be their friend.

He will shut them up in the closet and let them
    quit breathing.
He don't have to do nothing but sit in the yard all
    day long.
If they call him to come in, he won't hear them at
    all, and if they yell at him, he'll just laugh.
He won't do nothing, and they can't make him do
    what they want him to do.
He'll stick out his tongue at them, and tell them
    "no."
And he'll just play in the yard all day long.

This poem vividly describes the frustrations, fears, and hates that we have all experienced. Unfortunately, many of us carry these feelings with us into our adult life.

It looks as if the human condition and the structure of society cause many people to be deprived of their needs for care and comfort. All around us we see people who are protesting in every imaginable way that they failed to get what they needed when they needed it. Our hospitals are more than half filled by sicknesses of the mind rather than the body. Jails are filled to the bursting point and run a revolving door operation, spewing out two people and taking back three. Juvenile courts and detention centers are overwhelmed by sheer numbers. People can't stand each other or themselves. Many families are exposed to divorce or desertions among their members. Everybody has lost a friend or relative to suicide or drugs or alcohol. And those souls who manage to avoid becoming a statistic in the ledger of the courts, jails, hospitals, or welfare agencies—are they happy, mature, and comfortable? Hardly. Around me I see people floundering their way through life, seeking the care they failed to get. My colleague's secretary comes to work with a black eye that she got at home. A friend's adolescent boy has left home, and his parents don't know where he is or even if he is alive. A wife calls to tell me that the mild-mannered bookkeeper I speak to every day stays drunk at home, beats her and her children, and threatens to kill them and himself. My boyhood chum tells me he is leaving his wife of fifteen years and his three children because he's found someone who "really" loves him. A casual acquaintance at a meeting finds it necessary to tell me of his depression, his anxiety, and his fear of taking his own life. And my experience is not unique. All around us there are human beings who are protesting in violent, despairing, destructive ways that they need care, that they are afraid, that they are deeply resentful, and that they need help.

Maturity

My work as a psychologist requires me to try to be the kind of person who is helpful to others who are hurting. Certainly I can empathize and understand through my own experiences what it means to be overwhelmed with fear and despair. I know what panic and turmoil really are, and I know how guilt and depression can twist your guts as well as your mind. But knowing and sympathizing are not enough. I had to learn how I could use my experience to the advantage of others who were hurting. In my job I see children who can't learn, or can't manage to behave so that they can learn. I see kids who are smothered in fear and confusion. I listen to them and their parents, and I try to help them clarify their confused feelings and thoughts. I think about these people. I worry over them. I get angry with them. They get angry with me. And sometimes they get a better hold on their lives through what we do together.

My life and my exposure in a meaningful way to the lives of others have helped me understand and accept that when someone comes to me for help, I must be prepared to give and not hope to receive. My succor and pleasure must come from the other side of the fulcrum point of maturity where giving becomes as fulfilling as receiving. This is a feeling, a deep heartfelt conviction that is essential to me if I am to be of value to a sufferer. As Rosen puts it in his book, *Direct Analysis,* "The therapist, like the good parent, must identify with the unhappy child and be so disturbed by the unhappiness of the child that he himself cannot rest until the child is again at peace. Then the parent can again be at peace. If this feeling is present, the patient will *invariably* perceive it unconsciously."

Rosen here is describing the mature parent as well as the mature psychotherapist. They both have had their needs for security and comfort satisfied, either through the course of fortunate life circumstances or through the hard way— through suffering, rejection, and struggle that they have resolved by means of hard work, or perhaps by means of hard work and personal therapy with a mature therapist.

Unfortunately, not all parents or all therapists are mature. Many have unrequited needs themselves that they try to meet by borrowing from the resources of their patients or children. The parents we can do little about, since the requirements for entrance into parenthood are so easy to meet. We should do a better job in picking and preparing our therapists. As Rosen says, "Some people have this capacity for loving as a divine gift. But it is possible to acquire this the hard way—by psychoanalysis." Pick your parents carefully! If that isn't possible, be cautious when you choose a therapist.

Choosing a psychotherapist

It's really misleading to suggest that the average person chooses a therapist. It would be more accurate to say that this choice is thrust upon him in one way or another. His freedom in that choice is similar in kind to the freedom given us to choose our parents. And few of us have that privilege. If we are fortunate, we have good parents when we are born. When we are emotionally disturbed, we select a good therapist, if we are lucky.

Speaking from a limited, parochial view with admitted bias and restricted vision, I must say that I believe that most of the people doing psychotherapy as a major job responsibility are not equipped for the task. The formal study of most prospective therapists is filled with didactic content that has only a peripheral relationship to psychotherapy. Furthermore, the actual practice of the art under supervision during training is minimal and for the most part unsystematically directed. I have no proof of these assertions stronger than my observations over the years, added to the information I get from my associates and colleagues in meetings, conventions, and seminars.

I am convinced that the formal training of most novice psychotherapists has left them ill prepared to help a disturbed person. However, the major concern is, as I see it, in the personal characteristics of the helping person regardless of the strength, or lack thereof, of his formal preparation.

I see obviously aberrant, disorganized, disordered personalities in people who hold themselves out to an unwary public as psychotherapists. There's the hysterical social worker whose children have "dropped out," whose husband has left her. She's in the practice of "family therapy." Then there's my friend the guru. He's a clinical psychologist with years of experience. Now he's wearing a flowing sari, sandals, and hair from here to there. Interestingly enough, his bag is the alienated adolescent and young adult!

A psychiatrist of my acquaintance has his patients chanting and humming. They may sit in meditative silence with him for an hour or more at each session. Flashing lights, incense, and Oriental background music are apparently essential accouterments of his "treatment."

None of this is psychotherapy. Gullible people are being seduced with the promise of easy, painless ecstasy, of heaven on earth, of comfort and joy, if they will only believe. They are being misled and misused by therapists with more disturbed, disorganized, alienated personalities than their patients. Their treatment is their faith. You must be a true believer. And, sad to say, if you lose your faith, you'll lose treatment effectiveness.

The sane and mature therapist doesn't demand or need faith and blind obedience to achieve good results. He doesn't need or use magic, or exploit the immature remnants of his client's personality to achieve a worshipful, fawning relationship with those he would help. He doesn't use his patients to meet his needs before he attempts to meet theirs. He doesn't have sexual intercourse with his patients and rationalize his sensual use of someone as a "therapeutic technique."

To my amazement, I've found that sexual relations between client/patient and therapist are rather common in some circles. There are even appearing in the professional literature pontifical, weighty discussions of the ramifications of "love" therapy and its valid use in psychotherapy. Shades of ancient Rome! I get angry at such use and exploitation of suffering people. It's no big deal for the authoritative image of the therapist to convince the dependent, hysterical young housewife that her salvation lies in his sexual ministration to her. That's like shooting ducks on the water.

This is not to suggest that nuts, alienated personalities, and disturbed people cannot become adequate therapists. They can; many compassionate, effective therapists have severe emotional and life problems. But the outstanding characteristic of these therapists is that they have coped with their difficulties in a mature way, and they are growing with their experience. Their life's difficulties have contributed to their developing freedom, their empathy, and their ability to live realistically with their limitations and the world's adversities. The incense burning, chest beating, chanting head bangers and sexual acrobats have not. Their disturbance of personality is exceeded only by their avarice and their lack of regard for the sanctity of other humans. A few, of course, are quite sincerely committed to their behavior and convinced of its empirical validity. This only proves that the ability of the human mind to rationalize has no known limits or restrictions.

So if you need help, whom do you get it from? My advice is to follow the leadership of your stomach! If your gut tells you okay, then accept the man or woman who evokes that reaction and work with him or her. If you feel uneasy, if your gut says "no," then find someone else. My experience, my observations, and, thankfully, the research tell us that the best prediction of a satisfactory therapeutic relationship is the degree of empathy, or warmth and liking, between patient and therapist.

Beware of therapists who are curt and impatient with you. Avoid those whose habits and traits offend you. Be wary of any who require you to believe or behave as they do. Be cautious if he keeps his home phone and address a secret. Avoid him if he suggests you might get better faster in a prone position, especially if he's on top. Listen to the advice of your stomach and your heart. What do they tell you? Is he a phony or not? Is he for real—a genuine, honest, modest man or woman? Is he using you or letting you use him? If the room caught on fire, would he help you get out first, or would he bolt and run?

A good therapist should be well trained. It's relatively

easy to find out about that. He should be accessible to you in a reasonable way when you need him. His personal characteristics should resemble the description of the ideal Boy Scout. He really must be kind, brave, honest, and above all he must be prepared! I'm using levity to temper my inclination to be grim and ponderous about this issue. But I feel deeply for anyone who is seriously disturbed.

A good psychotherapist will be managing his own life satisfactorily even though he may have had considerable personal difficulty. He will show by his behavior that your needs are going to have first priority and his needs can be met after yours are fulfilled. He must be patient, but he must be demanding, firm, and convinced of the correctness of his methods and techniques. The good therapist will care in a nonpossessive way for you and for those things you feel are important. He will understand your thoughts and feelings most of the time, and when he doesn't, he will say so. He will be dependable, reliable, and always honest. He will be an open, nonthreatened person, but one who holds strong views on basic ideas. The effective therapist will demand that you work, and he will scold you if you don't. He will use whatever techniques he has at his disposal to help, and if his receiving abuse and scorn helps you, he will accept them. He will care, and his caring will express itself in anger if you persist in self-destruction. He will be real and genuinely himself, and his life will be a reflection of his therapy.

If, after repeated trials, you cannot find a therapist who suits you, consider the possibility that your hostility and anger and your ability to rationalize have blinded you to any valid qualities that anyone may have. Look at yourself and decide "who's right, me or everyone else?" If after reflection you determine that your thoughts and beliefs are valid and others' are false, then suffer; that's your privilege.

The group

7

AFTER FOUR YEARS of individual therapy, Carl and I were both
a little weary of each other. I seemed to have reached a
plateau in my growth and to be unable to go further. It
was clear to both of us that we had reached a stalemate in
therapy.

Carl suggested that I join an on-going therapy group that
he and a colleague, Glynn G., were leading jointly. This
group had a changing but relatively stable membership.
When one member felt well enough, or perhaps bad enough,
he left, and his place was taken by a new member; in this
case, me. At the time I joined the group, there were three
other men in it and three women.

I was late at the first session. Carl let me in when I
knocked on the door. With a brief expression of annoyance
he motioned me to a chair in a corner of the room. With
considerable anxiety I looked around; my senses were alert,
and my antenna extended.

A young woman is sitting in the other corner of the room.
She is sobbing quietly into a bundle of tissues. Around her
the conversation goes on as if nothing out of the ordinary

were happening. Occasionally when she sobs especially loud, some members of the group will cast furtive, hesitant looks in her direction. Unless she interrupts, the conversation continues around her and over her, but she will not join us.

Anna—the sobbing woman—is insatiable. She has to have the undivided, complete attention of the two group leaders. In those moments of attention she complains that she is always being "used." She is always giving and never receiving. If that is true, it is not reflected in her behavior here. After eighteen meetings of this once-a-week group, she has yet to make a comment that concerns someone other than herself. She can't give of herself. And sadder still, she is not ever aware that she never gives, that she only swallows up help and attention as a ravenous shrew gobbles up grubs.

In a few minutes she will stop crying. Her next remarks will provoke her laughter, which is unreliable, because it can turn to scorn and bitter contempt in an instant. Few of the group members dare respond to her cries: "What do you want me to do!" Any attempt to reply to this plaintive cry will be met with bitter rage.

It was fascinating, yet terrifying, to see Anna toy with her sanity. From week to week we could see her struggle to remain alive. She screamed and cursed; she raged and spat her venom at us and at Glynn and Carl.

"You son of a bitch," she screamed at Carl. "You don't give a damn about me; all you want is the money I pay you every week." It washed over Carl like a screen of fog. He was never perturbed.

Softly he replied, "If that's true, perhaps we'd better talk about the three months you have failed to pay for your group meetings."

Anna missed, or did not choose to understand, the

suggestion in his observation. Her hate was so strong that it almost overwhelmed her.

"I've got a gun," she said. "And I'm carrying it to work. If any of those bastards try to get me, they'll wish they hadn't. Nobody is gonna crap on me again. I've had it. The hell with all of you. You don't give me anything. Nobody gives me anything."

She raged away for minutes at each session until finally one day someone said, "You'd rather hate than love any day. But you're hating the wrong people. We should hate you. What do you ever give us but a lot of crap? All you do is tell us how helpless we are and what a bunch of bastards we are. The fact is that you're so damned mean you can't live with yourself." Somebody finally said what needed to be said.

Her anger exploded into a torrent of tears. She sobbed and gasped for breath until she was exhausted. After awhile she looked up and smiled. "Maybe you're right," she said.

I left the group while Anna was still struggling. I don't know what happened to her. She had a lifetime of hard work ahead. She was close to "losing her mind." And that term is almost literally descriptive. She teetered on the edge of chaos and destruction. Like most of us, she was bound to her self-destructive hate. It almost seemed as if her hate furnished her with something in life that was more satisfying and fulfilling than anything else she could hope for.

Who gets what?

Only one member of the group meets her challenge consistently, and that is Bernard. He admits that what motivates him is his jealousy over the amount and intensity of attention that Anna gets. He wants to be loved. But his pleas for love are received suspiciously since he is so quick to declare his unconditional love for everyone in the room (except Anna). I suppose that the group members feel that anything so easily gained is just as easily lost.

He is trained as a social worker, and he strives to be the official interpreter of the group. His comments glisten with psychological pearls such as "Oedipal complex," "castration anxiety," and "fixations." Instead of interpreting comments as he believes he is doing, he is merely labeling them. He was happy with a "newly discovered freedom," as he expressed it, when I first joined the group. But lately he has been morose and dejected. He says he has been more or less depressed since he was a child. His appeals for nurturance and succor are frustrating to the rest of us. The appeals seem so basic and so infantile that we despair of ever being able to fulfill them.

Only Buz seems hopeful. At least he verbalizes about hopefulness. But his declarations have the suspicious quality of whistling in the graveyard. He says he is hopeful about everyone except himself. I suspect that this is a thinly disguised gambit for some reassurance from us.

But Buz hasn't done well lately either. His pressing problem is impotency. It's troubled him intermittently for the past seven or eight years. Now, he says, it has recurred with the same old intensity. "Talk about sex," he says his wife told him. And he tries to talk. But he is rather curiously ignored. It's puzzling because he is a likeable, helpful man who is obviously gentle and sensitive. I wonder why the group doesn't respond more actively and positively to him? Buz is a history teacher in a local high school. He is apparently a successful teacher but unfulfilled by his work. The opening comments in the group are usually made by him.

Edward seems out of place with the rest of us and our problems. He never appears to be depressed or anxious. His comments are few, but they almost always are supportive or interpretative. He relaxes comfortably in his chair and regards us with a slightly bemused air. I sometimes get the feeling that he is an interested observer rather than a participant in the group. He has made only vague and veiled reference to the troubles that brought him here. One day while reassuring me about some remark he had made, he told me that he had suffered from an agonizing back pain which would not yield to medical treatment, but which has apparently been alleviated by group therapy. He really seems about ready to leave us.

Arnold and his wife, Gwen, are the only couple in the group. As Arnold put it, "My kids are driving me nuts." He's outspoken and moderately aggressive. We all like him. I suspect, however, that we are less able to empathize with his problems since his "kids" are twenty-two and twenty-five years old. Most of us are too young to have the separation problems with our children that his are experiencing. He's usually pretty quiet, but occasionally he'll blow up and cuss Gwen out. He seems to be almost begging her to respond in the same emotional tone. She refuses, though. Her replies and remarks are quietly stated and carefully emotionless. It is obvious that she is the family repository for all noxious emotions and guilt. She is the fulcrum around which the father-son battle rages. Her role is that of mediator, conciliator, and compromiser. She is not able to do this without considerable binding and expenditure of her own resources. This battle leaves her mildly but chronically depressed.

Arnold must have wanted another daughter. At any rate, he's adopted one in the group. He's always protective and kind to Betsy.

Betsy is rather shy and reserved. She looks as if she is trembling inside all the time. She reminds me of a frightened rabbit. You can almost see her twitch. When she talks, her voice breaks and trembles. She has had a recent spell of physical sickness which has been quite difficult for her. "I had to get up and get my own food while I was sick. My mother couldn't even fix me something to eat." Betsy's voice rose in a note of incredulity.

"Why didn't you tell her to fix something for you?" Arnold demanded. Betsy protested, "You shouldn't have to ask someone to feed you when you can't even get out of bed."

Then from me, "Maybe she was frightened and distraught by your illness?"

Betsy rejected that: "No, she wasn't. She just plain doesn't care." Her tone was resentful and remorseful.

I thought, "Good Lord. No wonder you're afraid and trembling—raised by a mother who won't even feed a sick daughter. How many other minor and major privations must she have suffered from infancy to now!" But Betsy must get something out of the situation herself. If she didn't, she'd tell her mother to get off her ass and get her something to eat. Her suffering is serving some purpose, some need for her.

Now Betsy says that she can't come back to the group. Her boss won't let her get off work early. She had changed jobs just a few months ago, and her previous boss wouldn't let her off early either.

"There are other jobs," insists Glynn, one of our two group leaders.

"It's just not that easy," argues Betsy. "I may be unable to work for several weeks if I have to have an operation. I can't just quit this job now."

Finally Anna asks for her, "Isn't there another group meeting at a more convenient time that she could attend?"

"Yes, there is," replies Carl, our other group leader. "But Betsy hasn't even asked about that possibility."

Betsy's crying now. She sobs, "Why should I ask? You've

told me I'm not interested or sincere about wanting help."
Bernard finally can contain himself no longer. "Well, why
don't you ask them? Go ahead, ask them!"

Betsy is sobbing now. "Okay, I'm asking." After several
uncomfortable minutes of silence Carl replies calmly, "We
have an opening in a Thursday evening group which should
be suitable for you."

We all breathe a sigh of relief except Betsy. She looks
trapped. Undoubtedly she had unconsciously hoped to ter-
minate group work. It is almost too much of a strain on her
already depleted resources. As we leave the room that night,
we each pause to wish her luck. We probably will never see
her again. But she has left a part of herself with us. We
weren't of much help. Perhaps the next group will succeed
where we failed.

Growing in the group

I was in pretty good equilibrium when I started group
work. But I have grown progressively worse as the weeks
pass. After six months I am chronically depressed with
sharp periods of agonizing despair lasting two or three days
at a time. For the first time in years I am forced to remain
at home on sick leave. Can it be my experiences in the group
that provoke these depressions? I know I am intensely frustrated much of the time. When I'm not frustrated, I'm
downright hostile and aggressive. Why do they keep insisting I remember my father? I can't! Nine years of my life are
gone. I can recall only one or two scenes from that period.
The rest is blank. I don't want to talk about it. It drives me
wild with frustration when they keep insisting I look back.
My remarks become more sardonic, more sarcastic, more
rejecting. The weeks go by, and depression sets in as if to
stay forever.

We meet again. I resolve to try again to express myself, even though the things I feel are likely to get me only further rejections from the group.

"Don't you see," I beg. "This is just the way I am. I just can't believe that all the corruption and crap in my feelings are caused by psychological factors. Who knows, it may be a little lump on a gland or a chemical imbalance that is causing this." Somehow I need to make them understand that it's not them I am rejecting, but an idea, a theory.

"I can see why you would have to feel that way," replies Glynn. "You've got to rationalize your rejection of us and what we're trying to do in order to maintain the only way of life you know."

Edward comments, "You would recognize what you're doing is plain resistance if you saw someone else doing it."

I regard him cynically and comment sarcastically, "So you've joined them." I point to our group leaders, Glynn and Carl. Silence for a moment.

Finally Carl says, "Have you ever wondered why you haven't joined us?"

Hoist by my own petard! I'm caught in my own logic. At last I begin to see, though only dimly, how resistively and rigidly I have held myself apart from them and the other members of the group.

"At last they understand," I think to myself. And I admit ruefully, I understand just a little that if I did really *join* them, I would have to give up my self-destructive behavior.

I begin to know—dimly, I can't quite perceive it clearly. But something does happen at that moment. I feel myself relax. I feel at peace. For just a few moments I am glad to be with everyone in the group. For just an instant we share ourselves with each other.

The goodness of that feeling lasts for two more days. Then it fades. My old familiar depression begins again. I have been failed again. My cynicism becomes stronger. My sense of hopeless despair leaps to my consciousness again. Can it be that I was just groping for the fragile straws of hope? Was that moment spurious? Can I ever really recapture the promise of peace that I felt at that indefinable instant when *something* happened to me?

Always poor

Tom and Linda sit next to each other. They joined the group just a short time ago. Linda lounges in a dreamy silence. Tom sits with his upper body thrust forward, hands clenched together. He looks like a caged animal. She looks like a defeated one.

"I don't know what I'm doing here," she says softly. "There's no way to change my life. I'll just go on and on until I'm crazy." The blank, fatalistic expression on her face frightens us all. Her words have the ring of prophecy.

We all rush to reassure her. "You'll be all right." "You can work things out." "Keep trying; we'll help you get to the bottom of it." Our words have a hollow, hopeless sound. We're afraid she may be right.

Tom looks pained and angry and bewildered. "What do I do?" he exclaims. "I have four rental houses I have to keep up, some property I'm developing at the lake, and a real estate business to run. It's all for you and the kids." He's genuinely perplexed.

Again Linda speaks with a quiet, deadly earnestness, "Did it ever occur to you that we need you? We need your body and your mind in the house with us."

"But I have to work. I have to make a living. We've got to have money to survive."

Linda looks at him for the first time. "Tom, who's surviving?" she asks.

The room is still and for a few moments we all think about what Linda has said.

Linda goes on in a low, almost monotonous voice, "He fixes the plumbing in the rental units, and we seldom have a toilet that works at home. He paints the house when the renter demands it, but our house hasn't been painted in eight years. I've wanted a rug in the living room, but I've never gotten one. When you're home you spend your time running around turning off lights to save money. How much will you have to have, Tom, before there's enough for us?"

Tom protests, "But if I don't spend my time making money, what will we live on? How can we pay our bills?" He's perplexed. Tom doesn't have the slightest clue about his wife's needs or what he is doing.

"Tom," Edward looks at him, "what Linda is trying to tell you is that no matter how much money you make, you'll always be poor." Tom doesn't understand that either.

In the weeks ahead, we would come to understand Tom. He spent a lifetime trying to "buy" the love of his exploitative parents who gave their approval only when he "earned" it. He had to produce before dad would spend a few minutes with him or before he could win an admiring word from his mother. He unfolded his life to us with many verbatim descriptions. We could clearly see and feel the cold, manipulative grasp of his parents on his life and his never ending, never quite satisfactory but desperate efforts to please, to win approval, and to be loved and cared for.

It was a revelation to me to see that he didn't have the slightest clue about all this. He couldn't see himself or what he was doing. More remarkable, he could not even sense the futility of his way of life. He tried to bargain. He tried to deal. "Well, maybe I could go along with you this far. Is that enough? Do I have to do more? How much more? Will you settle for this or do I have to do that?" He could not see that he could not bargain with his life and what he was doing with it. He had no idea of the forces that drove him or what he was doing to those who loved him. He remained a bewildered, harassed, and desperate man.

"Could that be me?" I asked myself. "If he can't see himself, then why should I see myself? Maybe I'm as blind as he is." At times, in brief flashes of revelation, I felt the truth of this. I really couldn't see myself or my style of life. I couldn't see what I was doing or what I was trying to win by my carefully controlled, but brittle, anger and resistance. The only guidance my life had at this point was provided by the strong conviction that I couldn't give in. Whatever that meant.

My sense of desperation grew. I was trapped, in pain, angry, and despairing. I felt I couldn't make it through another day, another hour, even another minute. "You bastard," I screamed silently. "Do something for me." Finally I said to myself, "Do something with me." I discovered I was speaking out loud.

Nobody in the group looked at me. They all seemed vaguely embarrassed. Someone put a hand on mine and squeezed it gently. Sobs grew in my stomach and climbed out of my mouth. I cried in utter frustration and misery. There was a long, miserable silence.

Finally Glynn said in an anticlimactic manner, "Our time is up for today." Everyone else stood up and with customary ceremony made his way out. I stayed.

"What can I do?" I implored Glynn and Carl. Carl put his arm around my shoulders. "I can't go on. There's no way I can go home tonight, and get up and go to work tomorrow. I can't stand it."

"If you can't stand it, I can have you admitted to a hospital tonight." Carl's voice was harsh in his frustration and exasperation. I know his patience was worn thin. After all, he had weathered crisis after crisis with me for several years.

I felt the critical importance of my decision at that point. If I gave up again, would I ever be able to come back? I had the feeling that my life hung in the balance at that moment. I didn't know what to do. I honestly doubted that I could make it another day without losing control of myself. The silence lengthened into eternity. I waited for something to move me—to determine my life and the course it was to take.

Glynn broke the silence: "I'd feel like kicking your ass if you gave up now." That was the voice I had been waiting to hear. Somehow, it seemed at that moment that he had the power to turn my course one way or the other.

So I said, "All right, I'll try again. Good night, I'll see you next week."

My life now might be quite different if nobody had spoken at that critical moment or if others words and other feelings had been voiced.

The depressive core

8

EACH LIFE is lived in congruence and harmony with its major and minor themes. Just as a tapestry is dominated by a recurrent, consistent pattern, so is a life characterized by dominant, repetitive behavior. Although the theme may be obscured at times or vague in outline, eventually it will reemerge to demonstrate its control of the picture and its association in a meaningful way of one part with another. This is a rather obscure way of saying something that we have all observed in the lives of people around us (although rarely in our own). The gloom and doom type of person will always find the situation threatening, the glass half empty, the life half over. The eternal optimist, on the other hand, will see the brightest possibilities in everything, will find the glass half full, and half a life left to be lived.

There is a constant, resistant inertia which guides us along our paths and this compelling force is difficult to divert even momentarily and almost impossible to change radically. The person who is dominated by the theme of hate will find things, circumstances, and people to hate. He will discover repeatedly and anew that others are capable of deceit, cruelty, rejection, and calumny. His living will reinforce his beliefs and his behavior will furnish him with an ever increasing array of proofs of the accuracy of his beliefs. Events and people who refuse to fit his mode of perception will be rejected or distorted if necessary. Promising events will be disrupted and friends will be alienated, furnishing further evidence that the theme of hate is indeed a valid one.

The converse, of course, can be said of the life dominated by love. When we act in love, we are returned in kindness and succor. Disastrous events provide opportunities for goodness and rebuilding. Trials yield new possibilities of our discovering strength and courage.

A new discovery

The discovery of these dominant themes in life is, of course, not new at all. What is new is the discovery by someone of the operation and strength and resistance to change of this in his own life! We can easily see that Aunt Susie is a complainer who would find fault with heavenly accommodations, or that Frowning Fred will meet rejection and discouragement everywhere he goes because that is what he is, rejecting and discouraging. But can we see that in our own living with our families and friends? Do we ever really recognize that the series of failures (or successes) in our lives is of our own making? Seldom. Rather, we have a rational and reasonable explanation for each job that went sour, each unfaithful friend, each unrequited love. Our contributions, if any, were negligible; it was always "their" fault or bad luck or an ill wind—never us.

The discovery of the operation of such a force in one's own life is more than half the battle in mastering it. It is relatively easy to change one's behavior. What is difficult is seeing for yourself that you must.

This is no more true for the reader than it has been for me. My life has been stretched along the twin patterns of hate and fear. Sometimes one is ascendant and then the other. But always the threads of one or the other have been woven through the tapestry of my life.

How do these themes become established? Where are the threads first picked up and when do they become clearly discernible as a living pattern? Probably early in life for most of us. They are made up of the minute and tenuous thousands of things that happen to and with us every day. The many smiles, the thousands of tears, the taunts and jeers, the help, the quip, the hugs, the cuffs, the joys and pains, the deaths and discoveries. The tapestry of our lives is woven of the threads of time and events. And it is made up of these by the untold millions. After a time the pattern becomes clear and fixed, and only monumental circumstances can serve to change its nature. However, many minor adaptations are possible and sometimes these may turn a so-so life into a good one, or a miserable life into a livable one. But it is essential that we *see* what kind of life we are making for ourselves if we are to change it.

Time frozen in fear

A major part of my life has been lost. When my father died I was nine years old, and my mind stopped in time. It was frozen in horror, in panic, and in rage. I had felt the growing panic through the course of his illness, but I didn't talk about it to anyone. I couldn't. I guess I hoped that if I didn't mention it, then it couldn't happen. I still often operate on that premise. As the weeks and months went by my panic and despair grew. But I didn't talk about it. One day my mother told me that I should know that daddy might have to walk with a cane when he came home because he might be crippled from the operations. I took this news impassively on the outside.

I was overjoyed. I had been afraid he would die, and now I was told that he would live. Walk with a cane. No problem there! Then she went on to say that maybe when he got home we could get on a train and go somewhere for a vacation. That furnished the material for many hours of contented autism. I visualized the three of us on a train; we were talking and laughing, mother in one seat, daddy and I (and the cane) in the other. We were together, and the rhythmic click of the rails and the swaying of the car lulled me to sleep many nights. Even now I love a train. It's a safe, pleasant place to be, and the soothing rhythm of clacking rails makes me feel easy.

But all reverie comes to an end, and so did mine. He died. My panic was finally realized. I was in a cataclysmic state of shock. My mother was heartbroken and hardly able to see my distress. I felt as if the earth was going to swallow us up. I felt alone, abandoned, naked in a frozen land. I thought that we would starve, die, be devoured. But I mastered this. I did it in a classic, distorted, self-defeating way. *I denied that he had ever lived.*

My mother later told me (twenty-two years later in fact) that shortly after the funeral I left her a note to the effect that she was to remove from the house all pictures or other items that in any way related to "him." I was nine years old at the time. From that day on until I was forced to change my life, I never mentioned his name, thought about him, or made reference to him in any way. Furthermore, if anyone said anything about him in my presence, I would leave the room. If someone expressed sympathy to me or mentioned fond memories, I turned and left without response.

Something should be there!

Soon he was gone. My mother was afraid to try to breach the wall I put up around me. My friends and relatives soon learned not to also. It was several years before I realized that I was expressing rage and hate for this man for having died and left me alone in the world. Now, that's stupid, isn't it? Hating someone for having died! After all, he couldn't help it, could he? But that's not the logic of a panic-stricken nine-year-old boy. In fact, that's not the psychological logic of us adults. We still react with some rage when someone we love leaves us, voluntarily or not. The old adage about a lover scorned is shown in its full power in death, which is the ultimate rejection.

So he left my life—in a sense. After a time I could not remember him at all. I have no fragment of memory of anything we ever did together, of sitting in his lap, of a present he gave to me, of going somewhere with him, of a kiss or a hug, or a romp, or a tease. I have nothing. And it still hurts me. As I write these words I am conscious of a huge, aching void where somebody and something should be. But he is gone. Even several years of analysis couldn't bring him back. However, it did bring back the ache, the fear, the rage, the hunger, and the still cry that tears through me.

It frightens me now that I'm a father. I have three children whom I love. The oldest is eight. We have been together many hours. We have had many, many happy times, many sad times. We have laughed, played, tickled, romped, and wrestled. Together we have read books, watched TV, and eaten many disorganized meals. We have kissed hurts, rocked and worried when they were sick, and spanked and fussed at them when we were impatient. How many hours, days, weeks? How many touches, caresses, kisses, hugs, and pieces of bubble gum? If I died today, would all of this be gone from their lives? The sheer horror of what I did to my father and to myself almost overwhelms me. Could I be banished summarily, regardless of merit, from the lives of my children? Could I be punished that way?

Every night in my prayers I ask God to bless my father. I have done that secretly for many years. I guess that is my feeble attempt to say I am sorry, that I treated him badly, that he didn't deserve what I did to him. I hope most of all that I can forgive myself. That's the hardest thing to do. I have forgiven him; that was the first thing I had to do.

So the threads of the pattern of the tapestry of my life came together to form an unchanging theme in my eighth and ninth years. Henceforth, hate and fear would be the dominant features of my living. True, these themes were muted and obscure at times, but they were always there and could always be seen by the careful observer. But not by me.

Expressions of rage

My hate was covert. It was manifested in sarcasm, in a quip, in subtle disdain, which the unsophisticated would interpret as genuine shortcoming in himself. I was quick to sense the possibility of rejection and quick to be the first to reject. I had to be asked. I had to be persuaded. I became an excellent critic, a good editor, a master of fakery, specializing in genuineness and sincerity. I used my friends' emotional needs as levers to drive them. I found fault, mastered the cool but polite technique. I invited confidences but divulged none of my own.

My fear was hidden. I mastered the art of impassiveness in the face of turmoil. I needed no help and asked for none. I could not seek or even accept kindness or pity. I was a clown, ready to play, anxious to have a party, the last to leave when it started, the teller of the latest jokes. I used the shock technique, said vulgar things that we all think, mentioned and made open hidden thoughts and unmentionable feelings. I was afraid of nothing, but I was afraid of everything. I laughed and laughed and sought out those who laughed too. I drank the wine and danced the dance. I denied my fear, my hate, and my despair until my denial could no longer be denied.

I hid my compulsive need to control people and things behind a facade of deliberate deceit. I felt aloof and disdainful of others, but I used them to signify and actualize my existence and worth. I felt rather like an actor before his audience. It didn't really matter who was out there beyond the stage lights, just as long as somebody was there who applauded and laughed at the necessary moments.

It's really amazing that I got along as well as I did for as long as I did. I made it in school because I was academically talented and I was an insatiable reader (that's something you can do alone in your own head). I didn't know what I wanted to do with my life. In fact, I didn't want to do anything with it. I wanted someone to adopt me and to take me and shelter me. I didn't know what I wanted to do, but I knew vehemently that I did not want to be a physician. It's curious to me now that I saw nothing psychologically strange in my over-reactive rejection of my father's profession, but I didn't. I suppose now that I would have elected to follow in his steps vocationally. However, that isn't really essential to my fulfillment either psychologically or professionally.

I guess as sort of an unconscious reflection of my own problems, I decided that the study of other people's emotional problems and processes would be the thing for me. And oddly enough it has been, although not for the reasons I imagined. I am quite sure that many people in the helping professions are there because of some conflict or confusion in their own lives that compels them to try to understand themselves. If they find approximate answers to these problems, they probably turn out to be pretty good helpers too. But beware of those who are still looking; they can ruffle your wig.

The price of changing

I have seen hate and fear in operation in my life in many ways. But discovering it once is not enough to enable you to do something about it. You almost have to rediscover it every day. And you must find how it manifests itself in its many devious and subtle ways. Then after you see this, you have to rediscover it again and again before you finally begin to believe it. Then, and only then, can you do something about it, which is the easier of the two jobs.

I have slipped and regressed and forgotten what I have learned. The price of changing is high, and the way to change is convoluted by many detours. I have to painfully drag my way back from each bypass. I have to look again at what I'm doing, what I'm feeling, and how I'm behaving, and then remind myself of what I have learned. I lie to myself, rationalize, and make excuses for the regressions. I backslide many times each day. But I look back, and I can see improvement. At the age of forty-two I am just through the developmental period of adolescence. At about sixty I guess I will attain adult stature, which is a little late, but for me that is progress.

At the hospital I was told that my major difficulty was with my dependency needs. This was true enough. The only problem was that it was about as useful to tell me that as it would be to explain the theory of electricity to a lightning victim. It made no sense to me in terms of how I saw my life and my problems.

It was at this point that I finally discovered the difference between intellectual and emotional insight. I used to think that this was psychological bull designed to cover up for the incompetency or obscurity of the therapist. But it really isn't. Intellectual insight consists of understanding and comprehending the concept in question. Emotional insight consists of believing it. For instance, my grandmother, a lifelong teetotaler, *understands* what a hangover is—that the hands shake, the head aches, the mouth thirsts—while I (having had a few) *know* what a hangover is.

The void of eight or nine years of my life is not easily filled. Let's face it, it will never be filled. Regardless of the insight I achieve (intellectual or emotional) or the behavior I successfully change or the feelings I successfully cope with, there will always be peculiar gaps in my personality structure, odd moments of atypical behavior, unusual needs for reassurance and approval, struggles with vague fears, and remnants of the fragments of a shattered juvenile world of stability and confidence.

Even now, or should I say especially now, I have moments of an irrational fear of a harsh, capricious fate. I'm afraid that through no fault of my own, my life will be shattered. When I sleep alone in a motel room far from home, I have fleeting moments when I see my wife and children swallowed up in a fire or set upon by robbers or laid out by a virulent disease. I have a mini-panic at those times and must remind myself again that this isn't real and that it probably won't happen again. For years I had similar fears for my mother, but now apparently I have shifted this focus of concern (which really is concern for my own well-being) to my family.

So I struggle with these and some other equally understandable feelings. But what do I use as experience to build feelings of basic trust, stability, and safety on when the building blocks of basic personality are, in my case, gone? How can I resolve my still unrequited dependency needs? Perhaps I have done so in the past by understanding and knowing where they come from and what form they take. I know I have resolved them in part by converting them into caring needs, which I satisfy by having my wife and children depend on me and by being able to satisfy their needs.

But in a way, I'm whistling in the dark, like a diabetic child who understands why he can't have candy but still wants it. I crave for a father to fill the empty years of my life. I want some good memories of a kind, strong, loving man who protected and cared for me. In my moments of need and despair, I'd like to remember my father when he smiled at me and talked to me and held me in his arms and said, "Everything is going to be all right."

On meeting loneliness

Man's most compelling, yet frightening, task is met in his attempt to reconcile himself to the fact of "essential" or primary loneliness. The discovery of joy is delightful. It is exhilarating when we share it with someone else. Our confrontation with loneliness is dreadful, but it is more bearable when someone else can be with us while we face it or when the onslaught of its darker side is overwhelming. But the critical nature of the experience of loneliness is that it can't be shared. We can be comforted in its presence. Love and tenderness and commitment can help us bear it and hopefully resolve its meaning for us. But these things are only philosophically incidental since each of us must feel for himself the grinding discomfort of essential loneliness and must then become aware conceptually that the state of loneliness is the disturbing factor, and then must reconcile ourselves to the compelling struggle to make this loneliness have a meaning in our lives. Hopefully this struggle will culminate in a serene resolution of what must be.

Undoubtedly there are people who never are really bothered by the desolate feeling of what I have characterized as essential loneliness. They probably are more to be pitied than envied. There are many more who are bothered considerably by it, but who never confront it fully or openly or successfully. Those who feel it, who confront it, but who fail in the critical third step of the task cannot reconcile this state of being, nor do they ever make of it an experience of growth.

Notice that I have not suggested that it must be finally settled or that any achieved reconciliation must be pleasant or happy. To the contrary, in fact, the confrontation and resolution of loneliness will more than likely be exceedingly painful; at times our strength to bear the awful realization of what loneliness must be is not adequate to the task. But when we finally are able to say, "I am alone in the face of death, of despair, of fear, of commitment and involvement; and I can bear this and I can make my life have meaning and humanness," then we have set the stage for meaningful growth to our ultimate limits of humanness. As Carl Rogers puts it, we are "becoming." A. Maslow, who has done considerable study of people who have successfully met these tasks, calls them self-actualizing people. And it seems to me that the successful confrontation with loneliness is the principal life achievement that these people share. Most of them have resolved this in the presence of great pain and personal anguish.

My own resolution of this stage of growth has not yet been successfully accomplished, if it ever will be. In fact, I am just now able to partially confront the awareness of loneliness that I discovered when I was nine years old. I didn't know at that time that I had entered into what for me has been a lifelong effort to avoid what I am now saying we must all face. I can recall it now for you, for you to use in whatever meaning it may have for your own struggle.

Fragments of memories of love and death

The first image I can bring to awareness of my father is this one. He is standing in the bathroom with his shirt off, his back bare, and his trousers dropped low on his hips. His friend, a druggist in town, is looking at his back, where there is a boil or lesion near the base of the spine. My father comments to the effect that he has tried to treat it himself, but it has failed to heal, and he's concerned about it. He goes on to say that he is going to see some doctor (Cannon?) in the city and find out what he thinks about it. I am eight or nine years old at this time, and this recollection constitutes the essence of my childhood.

The words of the psychoanalyst Kris seem pertinent here: "The traumatic significance of an event is not laid down from the time of its occurrence but . . . the further course of life seems to determine which experience may gain significance as a traumatic one." I have no doubt that if subsequent events of my father's short life had been different this brief scene would have faded into the waste heap of trivial memories. But those subsequent events were not to permit this.

He began a long series of operations and hospitalizations for spinal tuberculosis (commonly cured quickly today). I probably had been told of the seriousness of his condition. I know that I feared the worst. I was afraid that he was going to die and leave me alone. I know I didn't talk about this fear. Perhaps I couldn't. Perhaps my mother couldn't either. Or maybe I did and don't remember it any longer. I really don't know.

I must say that even now, thirty-three years later, in some dark recess of my heart, there lurks a cry that won't be stilled. A cry for what? What might have been? A cry of loneliness?

The days and weeks and months must have passed tediously and probably fearfully. I mercifully can't recall now. But several months of waiting finally culminated in a motel in the mountains one fall near the TB sanitorium where my father had come for care. My mother and I were there. We had been there several days, it seems to me. I remember that the man in the little café downstairs had some model airplanes that his son or nephew had made. He let me hold and play with them. To this day building and flying model airplanes evoke a feeling of comfort and security in me.

Then late one evening my mother said that we were going to see daddy. I don't know what I thought. Although I hadn't seen him for several months, I must have known what was to happen. But my mother and I didn't talk about it.

I don't remember going into the hospital. The next scene is in a large hospital room. It's an old but spacious and well-kept room, not really too clinical looking. Several people are in the room, which is semidark, like most hospital rooms. There are me, mama, two nurses, and the inevitable man in the white coat. My father is in a bed in the far right corner of the room as I walk in. His hair is white. It was black when I last saw him. He is gaunt and frail. His skin is translucent. He had been robust and ruddy. I can't recall what we said or how we said it. I think I remember that he told me of his love for me. I was stunned. I didn't know it then, but the task I was condemned to struggle with for the better part of my life had begun: the struggle with the awfulness of "aloneness."

I must have left the room soon; my mother wasn't with me. The next recollection I have is of crying and running down the middle of a long, curved driveway, lined on both sides by tall cedars or pines. It was dark, although a few lamps along the way cast a faint glow. The night was crisp and clear, and I can still see the stars glittering in the blackness of the sky.

I have no memory of the rest of our stay in those mountains. I guess such recollections are really superfluous anyhow. The essence of the experience of those months was contained in my run down that drive.

The human condition

9

WE ALL THINK egocentricly. "I am the only person who has ever felt this way." "I am the only person who has suffered like this." "I have to bear burdens that no one else bears." You are right too, in many respects. Only you can ever know what it means to feel just as you feel now. Only you will ever have experienced the terror and despair of the loss of love and care. Only you can know the feelings of hate and anguish, of love and hostility, or anxiety and peace that can exist at the same time in you, directed toward someone you value more dearly than physical life itself. As Kierkegaard puts it in his book, *The Concept of Dread:*

> But although there have lived countless millions of such "selves," no science can state what the self is, without stating it in perfectly general terms. And this is the wonderful thing about life, that every man who gives heed to himself knows what no science knows, since he knows what he himself is.

Other people have these emotions, in similar degrees and

circumstances. Yet in the final analysis, only you can feel what you feel, and only you can know the pain and pleasure of it.

We share some moments freely with others, but some of our moments cannot be shared, no matter how much we would like to. Eventually we face alone the most critical moment of loneliness, our first awareness of the personal certainty of death. But all through life we carry with us those tiny bits of sinking uncertainty, those brief lonely moments that we cannot share. Some people are apparently fortunate enough to view these instances with a minimum of anxiety. Others of us see them as terrifying shadows in the dark recesses and crannies of our beings.

You have felt the kinds of emotions I am talking about now. But it may never have occurred to you to look at what I call the aura of humanness, namely loneliness, as an essential characteristic of man. A characteristic shared by all persons, and therefore by you and me.

It has been said that the major difference between man and the animal is that man is aware of his "being" and consequently is aware of the certainty of someday "not being." It is this awareness with which we spend our lives and for which we structure our world. C. P. Snow said it well:

> the individual condition of each of us is tragic. Each of us is alone; sometimes we escape from solitariness, through love or affection or perhaps creative moments, but those triumphs of life are pools of light we make for ourselves while the edge of the road is black; each of us dies alone.

Then the search for "the meaning of life," which so many of us persist in, is doomed to fail. The existentialists, such as Sartre, have said that life has no intrinsic meaning, that we endow a life and make it meaningful, or ridiculous, only through our use of it. This then is to me a bare statement describing the basic human condition—"we have the opportunity and privilege to make of life what we will." Or we could phrase it another, more frightening way: "we are damned to make of our life what we will." This then constitutes our mission.

The discovery that we must give life its meaning can be, and usually is, overwhelming and terrifying for many of us. Yet this circumstance gives some people the opportunity to give meaning to their lives by helping others cope with and accept the "damning" human condition. These people call themselves variously counselors, psychotherapists, ministers, psychiatrists, psychologists, or perhaps mother, father, teacher, friend. It should be pointed out, however, that not all who are given these names are, except by vocational accident, fully committed to their responsibilities or their opportunities. Most of us have this task thrust upon us because of our needs or because of our concern for someone we care about deeply.

Caretakers: good, bad, and indifferent

Nearly everyone has the chance to develop a life "in his own image." Most of us have an opportunity to shape and mold another personality and to help it develop fully. Because most of us are parents, whether we have children who grow to be healthy and fully functioning beings or not is partially under our control. Some of us will reap a harvest of bitter disappointment and despair. A few parents will have children who grow to adulthood in a crippled, malformed fashion. Some of them will be crazy, some just peculiar, some antisocial, and some a violent danger to other people.

At the core of every neurosis, psychosis, or other emotional or psychological malady is anxiety. This anxiety can be exacerbated or soothed by life's circumstances. Whether or not it culminates in an overt and uncontrollable disruption of life functions depends on three factors: the constitutional strength of the person; the severity and chronicity of life stress; and the age at which unmastered stress was experienced.

The first factor, constitutional strength, is beyond our control or mastery. None of us can select the gene pool from which our organism will grow. If we are fortunate, we will inherit a stable nervous system and a sound physiology. If we do not, then we will be subject to the vicissitudes of misfortune in our physical functioning, including our nervous system, which may contribute heavily to our later inability to master excitation, frustration, and neglect.

The other two life factors, severity and timing of stress, are more open to modification. Although individuals cannot usually control these factors for themselves in their own lives, there are people in everyone's life who can.

Every child is born helpless. In his earlier days, his needs are few and relatively simple. He needs food, he needs water, and he needs warmth. There is growing evidence too that he needs physical contact and sensory stimulation. Babies who on occasion do not have these needs fulfilled react to this deprivation with rage and an apparent primal panic. If needs are met with relative promptness, rage and panic never develop; and if they do develop, they are rapidly extinguished.

As a baby grows, his needs for sustenance are expanded to items and acts that are extensions of these basic physical needs. Overt acts of love and caring are required to allay the feelings of anticipatory anxiety the child has for demonstrations of the continuing assurance that basic needs will be

met. In addition, these needs are extended to include factors
in life that are extensions of physical gratification. This is
the case when security, protection, and control of the environment come to be important to a growing child.

So it is from the basic needs for the literal requirements
of life-sustaining behaviors on the part of the baby's caretakers that all of our emotional and psychological requirements come. From this perspective then, you can see that
love, interest, caring, security, protection, control, direction,
sympathy, and a host of other reactions are equivalent, in
a primitive sense, to feeding, clothing, and sheltering. These
later emotional extensions of basic needs are merely elabo-
rations of the rudimentary life-sustaining physical requirements.

there is a difference b/w biological of non-biological for the child.

It is obvious then that the earlier disruptions or failures
to fulfill life needs are the most serious for the continued
growth of the child. And, of course, it is also evident that
they are the most difficult to treat therapeutically because
they form the basis on which psychological needs are elaborated (love, sympathy, comfort, interest, and so on) and also
because they are relatively inaccessible, since they usually
occur in the preverbal phase of the baby's life.

If we can accept this brief and simplified formulation of
life's psychological development, then we can easily see
that an early deprivation of basic needs is more damaging
than a later one and that a mild deprivation of an early need
may be as damaging as a severe blow to the fulfillment of
later needs. "When" becomes more important than "how
much."

All of these needs, early and later ones, are fulfilled
through human ministrations. Food and water don't fall
into the baby's mouth. Somebody puts it there. Relief of
discomfort and secure warmth don't occur naturally. Somebody provides them. And as a child grows, he knows in the

depth of his unconscious mind that it is a person, or persons, who literally give him continued life.

The primal fear

These facts (at least what I hold to be facts) establish the contention I maintain that the loss of life's protectors and providers is the most feared, most traumatic possibility in anyone's existence, and it is especially critical to the developing child. The loss of a protector (parent), then, is equivalent to the loss of one's own life. Psychoanalytically, to be neglected or discarded or abandoned by one's parents is equivalent to impending death. This possibility constitutes the core of anxiety for every child. He fears most of all the possibility of being abandoned in a world which will not supply his life's needs. This is why a four-year-old who is accidentally separated from his mother in a department store reacts with such primal panic. The unconscious specter of abandonment overwhelms him.

A child who does not have his basic needs met cannot grow with strength and certainty through the successive developmental periods of his life. Rosen in *Direct Analysis* puts it this way: "A child has to grow. If it has a parent suffering from a perverted maternal instinct, the child from the start must build on a weakened psychosexual base. Thereafter, at each critical period in development, the child will be shaken."

Most children, even those severely stressed, struggle on moderately successfully through successive developmental periods, although they may show clear signs of emotional distress. However, each succeeding period intensifies this stress. And, as Rosen explains, after years of stress and coping, the crippled child succumbs to a neurosis or even a psychosis—"the whole psychological structure crumbles back to what it started from, a shaky foundation."

So you can see that the parent who threatens a child with loss of love, either overtly or covertly, is evoking the most basic kind of terror that is possible. And the actual loss of a parent, through death, divorce, or psychological disability, is the most dreadful possibility in a child's life.

The parent who "holds back" from his child or fails to manifest his loving care causes the child to feel the threat of the loss of life needs and cripples him with the burden of chronic anxiety.

I do not believe that this formulation of the basic roots of psychological development is overdrawn or unnecessarily dramatic. It certainly applied absolutely in my life, and again and again in my practice as a psychologist I see children who manifest clearly their feeling of anxiety over the threat of abandonment.

One little boy of five was brought to me by his mother, a rather prim and stern lady, because he was having "seizures" in his sleep. He would scream and convulse his body and seem to be out of contact for ten to fifteen minutes with each episode. The attacks were occurring more frequently now, almost nightly. The neurologist could find nothing physically wrong with his nervous system.

I suspected night terrors from the description of the attacks given by his mother.

"Is John an angry boy?" I asked. "Does he fight with his friends frequently? Is he rebellious and resistive to you and your husband? What does his teacher think about him in kindergarten?"

John's mother reported that he did fight with other children at home and at school and that he had few friends because of his aggressive and hostile manner. "But," she said in a perplexed way, "he's like a different boy at home.

He never disobeys me or his father. He is quiet and does as he is told. His teacher says that he minds her too."

I asked if he ever ventured to "sass" or "buck" her or her husband. She replied in a stern, jaw-set voice, "He knows better than to try."

My play sessions with John revolved around the family members and interaction with them. His play was pedestrian and unremarkable until I introduced the theme of rebellion on the part of the boy doll. John was visibly shocked. When I had the boy shout to his father, "No, I won't do it! And I hate you because you're mean!" John nearly fell out of his chair in astonishment. In subsequent play sessions John spent the entire hour acting out themes of aggression and conflict between mother, father, and son. Finally, he even had a physical battle going on between them, which, incidentally, the boy won!

In about six weeks the night terrors disappeared. His mother was happy, but she was concerned that John was getting to be a little "lippy," as she put it.

It seems clear that John had occasional intense feelings of hostility and rage toward his mother and father, which is natural, since every "normal" child has periods of alternating hate and love for his parents. However, John's parents tolerated no evidence of hostility from their child. I don't know what they did that made him repress these feelings. However, I imagine that they conveyed subtly, through their stern, cold, demanding manner, that John faced the possibility of lost love if he didn't curb his feelings. Consequently, John's fear of the feelings of hate exploded in unguarded moments in sleep in the form of terrifying nightmares.

Remnants of childish feelings about aggression, authority (parental love), and the possibility of loss of love are present in every one of us, no matter how old or mature we may be. If these feelings were handled in a healthy way during our developmental period, then such reactions contribute to our living by making us compassionate, loving, and caring persons. If these needs were subverted, we are vulnerable to life's stresses, especially those frustrations that are psychologically equivalent to a loss of love.

This is why acts of independence have been so traumatic for me. Of course, stages of increasing independence carry with them the corollary of less support and less caring from the people who give us our emotional sustenance. Now it is easy for me to understand why going to college, joining the armed forces, getting married, and earning a doctorate were periods of such severe stress for me. They represented decreases in support and increased expectations of independence.

The saddest thing about this whole matter is that immature, unsatisfied people (like I was?) have children and cannot "feed" them the emotional fare they need to master their own development. On the contrary, some of these parents try to get their children to "feed" them instead. And so the circle of hungry despair is unbroken.

Is there really a Santa Claus?

I suppose that everybody, no matter how old, harbors in his secret and deepest feeling the hope that there really is some magic in the world. "Perhaps," we whisper to ourselves, "events are not really determined." "Maybe, just for me, nature's laws can be overruled." "Perhaps lady luck will rest her hand on my shoulder and I will receive unexpected and unearned riches and blessings." "Somehow, just this once, I will not have to pay in life's coin for what I get, or don't get." "This time I may not have to work for my supper. Somehow, somewhere, just maybe I won't have to pay the going price for what I want."

No matter how mature we are, we still carry remnants of

the belief in magic that we learned in our infancy. After all, it was magic then. When we cried, somehow we were miraculously fed. When we were wet, someone dried us. Hurting was soothed and loneliness dispelled. And all of this for nothing from us. We just screamed our displeasure, and behold, things were made right.

As we grow older we learn that things don't really just happen; someone or something causes them to happen. We get our help from others or we earn our rewards and fulfill our needs through our own efforts. In other words, we pay by our actions for the things we get. We learn also that sometimes we must wait, even though we want something badly. Or we even learn to tolerate the idea that we may not get what we want at all. We learn to endure pain and to tolerate discomfort and disappointment. Most importantly, we discover that we must actively work to get what we need, be it objects like cars and refrigerators and food, or emotional sustenance like love and companionship. But in our heart of hearts we still maintain vestiges of the hope that the conditions of our childhood will come again, and we will be succored and cared for whether we do anything for ourselves or not.

Of course, most of us recognize the childish appeal of these feelings and indulge in them in a half playful way by such actions as buying a lottery ticket or "knocking on wood" or "wishing on a star." When we are tired or disappointed or afraid, we may daydream and fantasize even though we know full well that we really are adults and that our fears and hopes will not be quieted or resolved by any miracle. The less mature among us continue to believe that magic will solve our problems of living, and that somehow, through no effort on our part, our trials and tribulations will be eased. Such people are not tolerant of delay. They want what they want now. They feel that other people should serve their needs and that others are there primarily to still their fears and feed their egos. They are angry if their needs are ignored or if fulfillment is delayed. They walk around with a perpetual chip on their shoulders, angry at a world that demands that they pay for what they want.

A number of industries have grown up around the adult's remnants in his personality structure of childish needs. These industries exist to gratify our inability to tolerate delay and to soothe our resentment over the demands of nature for effort in exchange for gratification. Some of the more unimportant evidences of this are seen in our propensity for instant service. We have instant coffee and minute rice and quickie divorce. We have blue stamps, red stamps, and green stamps, all of which suggest something for nothing. We have fortune tellers, astrologers, and horoscopes. We ask for special evidence of unusual favor from these kinds of people, and some of us even believe that they may know the secrets that will enable us to recapture the magic we once had.

At a more sophisticated level we find the "wish for magic" phenomenon periodically renewed in what we would normally consider to be scientific, rational, objective people. As evidence of the continuing power of this phenomenon, even in professional people, we find serious consideration of such things as psychic powers, extrasensory perception, sorcery, and witchcraft. And then, blending into the realm of objective evidence and rationality, we find a serious involvement of otherwise mature people in meditation, yoga, and drug trips.

Freedom found

For instance, just recently a lady came into my office to seek support for a proposed "research" project. She introduced the subject by reviewing her life history in considerable detail, emphasizing how she had been beset by fears and troubles. She reported that she had been hostile and angry and ineffective in her job. Now, everything was solved. She had begun transcendental meditation and lo, she was calm, full of confidence, creative, open to other people, friendly, free of worry; she slept well and was not even distressed when her husband died recently!

When I indicated that I knew little of meditation and had no great interest in it, I immediately saw that I had made a serious mistake. This calm, open, friendly woman berated me at length for my narrowminded rigidity. She questioned my competency, my integrity, and my ancestry. When she left me, she was a seething, burning, offended "true believer." If I had not known better, I would have thought I was talking to an angry, hostile, rigid person.

Such people want something for nothing. In this case, she wants peace of mind and psychological security without paying the price of working to know and to understand others and their needs and herself and her needs. She wants peace at bargain basement prices. This phenomenon is seen with encounter group adults who believe that one night of "open" expression of their feelings and toleration of others will bring instant nirvana.

The old hope for magic surfaces again and again. "By chanting some secret incantations and achieving a oneness with my mind, I'll be free of the frustrations that beset my life." Or, "One nude marathon group focusing on my hopes and fears will free me of my hate and despair." "Could it be that drugs will introduce me to a new state of consciousness where I can see new beauty and a new kind of truth?"

Even scientists are subject to abandoning their science if they can delude themselves that magic is still a possibility. Witness the current interest in acupuncture by physicians.

It's as if the phenomenon of suggestion had never been discovered. All are hopes for magic. And all will prove to be disappointing and barren unless such a search is accompanied by a willingness to take the hard, high road—the road strewn with the rocks of self-denial and twisting and turning through the detours of fear and frustration. The hope for the easy way lives on, but it leads to deeper despair and increased self-deception.

True, one must look inward. But one must be willing to take what is found and use it in life's living. The real mastery over life will come to those who take their suffering and fears into the world and who deal with them realistically from the time they rise in the morning till they lie down at night. We must confront and challenge our secret fears. We must endure our frustrations and refuse to visit them on others. If we are free and open, we don't have to tell everyone about it. They will know it. And if we must exercise our independence and freedom, we don't have to grow hair to our waist to prove it. Freedom lies between the ears, not above or below or outside of them.

If we are free, we can permit others to be in bondage if they insist on it. If we are at peace, we can grant others the right to be in turmoil. If we have no fear, then we cannot be afraid of those who don't believe as we do. Most important of all, if we are loving, we can foster love in those close to us.

Childish needs and childish ways

I cannot document or otherwise prove that my contentions regarding the lifelong effects of childhood deprivation or trauma are universally true. Perhaps they are not. I know only that such has been the case in my life.

As I look back on the psychic scars left by the loss of my

father and the chronic fear and hostility that this engendered in me, I can see clearly how certain pivotal points in my living have been markedly affected. My life was a series of ups and downs coinciding with episodes when I was threatened with a loss of support or required to exercise independence in responsibility for myself.

Each of my depressive periods coincided with an instance when I had to extend myself beyond my family and "act like a man." For example, I can recall vividly the difficulties I experienced when I left for college, went into the navy, accepted my first professional job, got married, entered a doctoral program, and reached the point of postdoctoral employment.

From this vantage point, it is easy for me to see that each of these instances was an occasion when I "left the nest." Psychologically I reacted to them as abandonment and loss of nurturance and protection. The more mature and demanding the occasion, the more traumatically I reacted. Emotionally I always felt as if I were alone in a hostile world. I had the gut feeling that I would be left to die. My reaction was cataclysmic and panicky. I could not be consoled or reassured. Deep inside I was afraid and tortured by a primal, indefinable dread of destruction and loneliness.

This reaction was characterized—prosaically, I thought—by the psychiatrist at the hospital as due to unresolved dependency needs. That sounds so innocuous and scientific that it's no wonder it made no particular sense to me then. It surely does now. Now I know that "unresolved dependency needs" can culminate in a raging turmoil of panicky depression and desperation and that the color of our life's fabric will be determined by our success or failure to recognize and live with the unmet needs of childhood. It is indeed a fact that "the child is father of the man." The further away I get in time and psychological distance from this turmoil in my life, the clearer I can see the fear-stricken child in me, desperately trying to cope with the felt certainty of despair, abandonment, and destruction.

We all have remnants of these feelings and fears in our lives. Some have more than remnants. But even those of us who are reasonably "normal" experience something of these emotions when we lose a friend or relative to death, or when we are forced to move to a new town and give up our familiar surroundings and our colleagues and acquaintances. This primal reactivation of childhood needs makes a job loss in middle life a devastating experience for some people. And it is not the threat of economic loss alone that accounts for our reactions to being fired or laid off. We see similar reactions in people who have to retire. Many of them respond as if they were abandoned and lost. The folklore regarding the rate of premature deaths in retired persons is a documented truth. Suicide is common in older people who no longer have the security and protection of a job and the comfort of relationships with fellow workers and business friends.

Most of us never consciously recognize such fears, much less connect them to childhood frustrations. Instead, we rebel against our feelings in nonproductive and indirect ways. We drink too much and party too long. We work too hard and too compulsively, or conversely, we find it difficult to work at all. We malign and antagonize those we work with. We are resistive and passive, or hostile and uncooperative. Of course these feelings spill over into our relationships with our families and friends; we are impatient with them and intolerant of their needs and welfare. We are short-tempered, ill-natured, and sometimes physically and psychologically abusive. In short, we act like tired, fearful, petulant children. In reality, that's what we are.

What it means to feel

10

I GUESS you have time to think in any hospital. In a mental hospital you have far too much time to think. Most of us neurotics do far too much introspection anyhow. Certainly I was no exception. I tried to penetrate the "blooming, buzzing" confusion of my own swirling, convoluted feelings and impulses and thoughts and fragments of feelings. With predictable and repetitive consistency my mind turned to my feelings. "Are you happy or sad, elated or depressed, excited or afraid, anxious or serene, joyful or despairing?" "Are you all of these things?" To me, feeling was synonymous with life. So I thought a lot in those weeks and months in the hospital about my own feelings.

It's difficult to talk about feelings and emotions. Noncognitive aspects of behavior have been conceded to the artists, the philosophers, and the poets for study and explanation. Such professionals as psychologists and psychiatrists, supposedly concerned with human behavior, have done little to help us understand emotional life emotionally. We know something about it intellectually. *Feeling* really is the essence of life, not *knowing*. If discussed at all, emotions are described in terms of behavioral manifestations which are their derivatives rather than their essence. This doesn't hold true for all psychologists. The humanists and the existentialists are concerned about becoming articulate about humanness. Those counselors and psychotherapists who are able to expose themselves fully and openly to the people they are trying to help are coming close to what is important in existence. These are the people I characterize as having understanding and sympathy. And I mean sympathy in its broader, not its bleeding heart, connotations. Kierkegaard described it this way: "Sympathy one must have; but this sympathy is genuine only when one knows oneself deeply and knows that what has happened to one man may happen to all. Only thus can one be of some utility to oneself and to others."

When one is compelled to deal only with behavioral manifestations, much of the meaning of human events is lost. I think of myself lying there in that hospital bed that first night. Behavioral description: "rapid pulse, hyperventilation, rigid musculature, easily startled," and so on through the minutiae of all possible physical observations. But you and I know now how little that tells of the man whom I have described on this important night.

Observations such as this, without the tempering of feelings as the acknowledged essence of the human experience, are of limited value only. For instance, one crucial dynamic sign of the disorder termed schizophrenia is blunting or dulling of affect. By this psychologists mean that the patient presents a rather bland, unconcerned countenance and in discussion he seemingly has little interest or involvement in surrounding events. He seems detached and uninvolved. This kind of description and interpretation is of limited help and offers little aid in understanding what is important in this condition.

Let me try to explain it this way. The sufferer is so over-whelmed with sporadic waves of psychic pain that his at-tention and efforts are consumed in girding his being to cope with the next onslaught. In spite of the intentions of the sufferer, something inside him demands that the next wave of pain be met and the struggle for survival be renewed. Under these circumstances, what do you expect? Feeling is blunted, but only toward those outside events which are of limited importance to the sufferer. Oh, that all feelings were blunted! Mental patients with some insight and a measure of psychological knowledge find the solemn diagnostic blunting "sign" amusing. That is, they find the interpreta-tion amusing. The blunting and dulling of affect and the seeming internal preoccupation are the results of violent, virulent feelings that are lashing about uncontrollably in-side.

Did you ever try going to a party with a severe toothache? If you have, you have some small notion of what it's like for the seriously emotionally disturbed. He has little energy available with which to appear interested, amused, con-cerned, or involved.

The cowardly ones

Someone once said that the bravest people in the world are neurotics. I think that this is true of everyone who suffers some serious and chronic emotional turmoil. The vivid imagery and lush fantasy life of the sufferer would, I am sure, stagger the comprehension of our "normal" broth-ers.

The sufferer conjures up a monster in the midst of para-dise, thirst in an oasis, death in the birth of life. He spends many of his waking and most of his sleeping minutes in a disquieting struggle with bad luck, illness, natural and man-made disasters, and never really succeeds in prevailing over these noxious things. The imagination can always come up with stronger terrors when the milder ones are mastered or lose their temporal significance.

Then the sufferer has to do double, no, triple duty. He has to cope with life just as you do: real life with its problems and joys, with its sorrows and despairs, with its bills and car repairs and wrong numbers. But he also has to struggle with the problems that his mind conjures up by day and with the monsters that his subconscious spews out by night. Yet in spite of this enormous expenditure of energy, he is often a compassionate and understanding friend and frequently a prodigious worker. I suspect some administrators look for the most compulsive nut they can find for some of the really "dirty" jobs that have to be done at the office or the clinic or in the stockroom. This sufferer may have the kind of compassion that makes him of use to his fellows. Kierkegaard describes it this way:

> Compassion is so far from being an advantage to the sufferer that rather by it one is only protecting one's own egotism. One dare not in a deeper sense think of such trouble, and so one spares oneself by compassion. Only when the compassionate person is so related by his compassion to the sufferer that in the strictest sense he comprehends that it is his own cause which is here in question, only when he knows how to identify himself in such a way with the sufferer that when he is fighting for an explanation he is fighting for himself, renouncing all thoughtlessness, softness, and cowardice, only then does compassion acquire significance, and only then does it perhaps find a meaning, since the compassionate man differs from the sufferer for the fact that he suffers in a higher form.

Now I think we have some sense of the compassionate in

contrast to the sympathizer. Marx and Lenin were sympathizers. Christ and Gandhi were compassionate.

The sufferer may become compassionate if his search for humanness is fruitful. But while he searches he suffers exceedingly. He sometimes gets up in the morning when a man of lesser courage would lie there moaning. He works at his job with only half the mental and physical resources that are available to the "free" man. The rest of him is busy—busy battling the terrors his mind spawns. He smiles when a cry would be more appropriate. He volunteers for extra work because he must not doubt himself and his worth (or worse still, have you doubt him). He tries to control strong, unreasonable feelings, unwanted anger, unknown fears.

Sometimes his body lets him down. His stomach may spew its contents. His bronchial tubes constrict, making breathing difficult. Veins in his skull constrict and his head throbs. His intestines writhe and his bowels rebel. His skin may erupt or his ears ring. His hands may become unsteady. His heart races or skips or sickeningly thuds. But he learns to cope. To do so requires another exceedingly difficult series of adaptations. Drugs, rigid schedules, denied pleasures, protection from noxious circumstances and tasks (which become so frequent and numerous that they are hard to avoid)—all of these devices are used and sometimes, almost always, they eventually fail. In spite of the ingenious devices that the sufferer manages to use, the all-pervasive emotion we call anxiety is still lurking somewhere, waiting for a renewed chance to attack.

Many books have been written about this emotion. Many dramas, fictional and real, have revolved around it. Concepts of life have attributed to it a generic, motivating force. Attempts to deny its power are continuous. But anxiety remains the king of the jungle of destructive emotions.

Kierkegaard described it definitively in *The Concept of Dread.* He uses the word *Angst,* which is roughly comparable to the psychological terms, free-floating anxiety and existential anxiety. His translators use the word dread.

> Dread is the possibility of freedom. Only this dread by the aid of faith is absolutely educative, consuming as it does all finite aims and discovering all their deceptions. And no Grand Inquisitor has in readiness such terrible tortures as has dread, and no spy knows how to attack more artfully the man he suspects, choosing the instant when he is weakest, nor knows how to lay traps where he will be caught and ensnared, as dread knows how, and no sharp-witted judge knows how to interrogate, to examine the accused, as dread does, which never lets him escape, neither by diversion nor by noise, neither at work nor at play, neither by day nor by night.

This Grand Inquisitor, so well described by Kierkegaard, is always on duty, always ready to renew the interrogation. And not only can the sufferer not escape continuous confrontation with him, he can rarely convince himself that he will ever find respite.

In the world afraid

And where does dread or anxiety come from? Do some of us just naturally have more of it than others? Are some of us destined by our fate to have so much of it that we cannot live?

Anxiety is the common denominator of emotional distress and disorder of all kinds. Happy, comfortable people don't just "go crazy." Crazy people have literally been "driven crazy." They have come to a point in their lives when they can no longer contain or control the rampant fear, panic, and rage in their minds, and they become disorganized and disoriented. However, looking at it from the perspective of the crazy person, the behavior we see is really not strange at all. It is rational if you grant him the validity of his fear or rage. If, for instance, the world were really a hyperthreatening place with the possibility of attack from any quarter at any time, then it would make perfectly good sense to hide from strangers, to isolate yourself, or to call the police to protect you. The behavior is rational; it's the belief about the world that isn't.

Emotionally disturbed people are threatened people. They react to fear and threat with rage, hostility, and aggression. Since these noxious feelings are rejected by the conscious minds of most of us, they are repressed. Repressed emotions must emerge in some form; and for some unknown reason, attributing our own feelings, motives, and ideas to someone else when they are unacceptable to us is a common human behavior.

So if my life has been dominated by fear, or if I believe it has, then I will react with feelings of rage, frustration, and despair. Since I cannot accept that I feel this way about others, I make a simple shift in emotional logic and "give" these feelings to others. Now it is they who are filled with hate and venom. The circle of psychological logic is complete. The formulation thus becomes: "People around me are hateful and cold. They have no love or even tolerance for me. They are resentful and impatient with me. Nobody is willing to help me; if I fall down, I'll be stepped on. If I'm starving, nobody will feed me; and if I hurt, nobody will comfort me."

Of course it follows logically that if I see this kind of world with these kinds of malevolent people in it, I'm crazy if I'm not crazy. Who wouldn't be afraid in this jungle? And this is the way the emotionally disturbed person feels about his world. How long it takes him to "go crazy" depends on how much trauma he has endured, how early in his life he began to suffer, and the kind of support he gets from others who are important in his life. Another factor which we know far too little about concerns the constitutional factors and attributes of the person in terms of hereditary qualities. Undoubtedly, constitutional factors play an important role in determining the quality of our emotional life and our psychological well-being. But how and by what means and processes we really know too little.

But what is this trauma that we speak of? What is it, and where does it happen? I will discuss this more completely later.

Learning and feeling

John Rosen in his book, *Direct Psychoanalysis,* says that there are two ways to reach maturity. The first, according to him, is by "divine grace." By that he means that we can grow to be emotionally mature if we are nurtured by parents who themselves have attained secure adult status because their needs were met in their growing. Such persons also have the good fortune to have had a secure childhood life and to have escaped such misfortunes as parental desertion, death, divorce, or economic deprivation. These fortunate people have had a good school experience and sound physical health, and have been spared life's capricious calamities such as accident, war, or hereditary disorders. In short, some lucky people reach the stage of adult emotional and psychological maturity because they had stable, mature parents, and were afforded a secure, need-fulfilling childhood.

Many of us were not similarly smiled on by the gods. We were not given what we needed to make the passage through our developing years a smooth and pleasing journey. Our lives were disorganized and disrupted, disturbed and damaged. Some of us suffered the effects of parenting by men and women who themselves were afraid, embittered, and discouraged. More of us felt the strains and agonies of parental divorce or death. Some of us were the unintended victims of suicide or alcoholism in those who were to furnish us with our emotional food. A few were crippled by disease or accident or by other circumstances which blunted their capacity to grow and stunted their developing minds and feelings.

Unlike the recipients of "divine grace," who grow to be loving and free people, life's victims have a much more difficult time in reaching a satisfying level of emotional and psychological maturity. Many never reach anything like a satisfactory adjustment to their needs and life's demands.

What can we do for ourselves if we are among the unfortunate ones? Does this mean that a disturbed childhood and unfulfilled needs doom us to live miserably and to pass this regrettable, tragic legacy on to our own children? Rosen says that there is another way to reach maturity: through psychoanalysis.

Now I am certain that many would quarrel with Rosen that psychoanalysis is essential for the repair of the damaged personality. It would probably be more acceptable to say that people with problems of arrested personality development must struggle to obtain the comfort and growth that come naturally to others. The fashion in which this struggle is engaged may indeed take the form of psychoanalysis. But it may not.

Psychoanalysis can provide me with a meaningful way to see myself and to understand what forces are acting on me. The supposition is that when I see myself realistically and understand why I behave as I do, I am able to change what I do and abandon old, destructive ways of behaving. However, any kind of personal therapy that has as its aim growth in self-understanding can accomplish the same purpose. This is why some people are helped to lead fuller, more satisfying lives through such therapy as client-centered or nondirective, group counseling, Gestalt, rational-emotive, and a host of other varieties of uncovering therapies. On the other hand, the same reasons doom the techniques that aim solely (or primarily) at emotional catharsis or focus solely on feelings as a lasting way to personality development.

It is extremely difficult, if not impossible, to "see" oneself, for oneself, by oneself. We cannot see our own resistances, blind spots, and rationalizations. If we could, we wouldn't be disturbed and unhappy. We would have long ago cured ourselves. No, it is necessary to have someone who can help us in a firm but sympathetic way. Those who help us must be sympathetic to earn our trust and confidence and must be able to understand how we hoodwink ourselves in order to maintain our precarious balance, and they must be firm in the face of our self-directed lies and our desperate attempts to cover up and retrench. Above all, they must be patient and know with an understanding that comes from personal experience that we are compelled, that we must resist and retract, and evade and deny. In the face of these tactics, the good therapist helps us to carve out small steps along our way and to accept the fact that progress toward maturity is a slow, painful, and erratic journey.

Carl Rogers in his paper, *Learning to be Free,* characterizes this process as a groping toward freedom and maturity. He says, "The client moves gradually toward a new type of realization, a dawning recognition that in some sense he chooses himself. This is not usually any sudden burst of insight—it is a groping, ambivalent, confused and uncertain movement into a new territory."

Rogers goes on to explain that although it may be true that we are products of our past, we do not have to remain history's prisoners. We can change life's circumstances and use our strength to become what we would be. We can become persons who choose rather than robots who react. But first it is necessary for us to finally realize that in our misery we are truly driven, that we are not making choices but living in duplicity and anxious deceit. When we can really see that we are driven by internal forces and external pressures and are not really free to make our own decisions and choices, then we are finally ready to begin the struggle toward self-direction and growth.

My treatment in the hospital certainly has not led me to these conclusions about learning to feel and to be free. However, the experience of learning the remorse and agony of not being free has taught me something. My freedom was not extended by the hospital stay or anything that happened there. But my compassion and empathy for the suffering of others were.

Beginning again

11

WHAT WILL LIFE BE for me? I don't really know. I often have the feeling that the proper response to this self-directed question is that I haven't decided what is to be. This probably sounds strange coming from someone who sees himself as a "victim" of a mental disorder. I am in the paradoxical position of feeling that I am both the victim and the perpetrator. Somehow, I feel I can control some of the things that I think and do, but I feel partially at the mercy of an inner battle for control that is going on between mysterious forces that I only dimly perceive. I want that part of me that is happy, confident, secure, that is open and warm and accepting, to prevail. But will it? There is a malignant part of me that is fearful, hostile, despising, that is cruel and dangerous. It may finally prevail.

In my darker moments, it is the tenacious persistence of this malignant part of me that I am afraid will determine my ultimate fate. At those times I wonder, "Why continue to fight?" Like the armies of China, my foe is too many. As quickly as one of them dies, two more are ready to replace him. Yet, I am beginning to believe that this fight must have an objective that transcends mere defense. In other words, it is not enough that I resist the persistent attack of those "dark" forces. This is a fight I may continue until I die of senility. But I can never win in such a manner. I am coming to believe that somehow, sometime, I must commit myself to something. Now that probably sounds strange. "Commit myself to something." But I never have. My life has been a long series of isolated struggles against those things that would overwhelm me. It has never been a life of a commitment to a positive goal—a goal which transcends "the struggle against." Besides, I don't know that this goal has to be especially glamorous or publicly laudable. It will probably be quite modest.

Then why do we hurt?

People cling to their misery and pain. They embrace despair like an old friend. They nurse hatred as if it were their child. It has taken me some years to realize that, for the most part, a person makes his own pain, and furthermore, he will vigorously resist efforts to take it away from him. In the face of incontrovertible evidence proving the effects of our actions, we refuse to abandon behavior that is destructive and feelings that cause us agony.

This doesn't make sense. It's not logical at all. If you saw a man pounding his head with a hammer and crying in pain, you would assume that if you pointed out to him that his head was hurting because he was hitting it with a hammer, he would stop. But you would be wrong. He wouldn't because the satisfaction he was getting from hitting his head would be greater than the pain it caused. In fact, the resulting pain may be serving to punish someone else.

In my own life and in the lives of others I have observed in group therapy and have tried to help in therapy myself,

I am constantly amazed to find that a person will persist in destructive, painful behavior and will resist every effort to get him to abandon it. The common plea is, "Change me so I don't hurt, but let me continue to act and feel as I do now." "Change *me,* but don't tell me to change my behavior." They really don't seem to grasp, as I didn't for so long, that we are what we do, nothing more and nothing less. We cannot act in a hateful and cruel way to others and feel loving and kind. We can't hate and harbor old grudges and resentments and be sympathetic and open. Worst of all, we can't behave in hurtful ways and provide those we love with the freedom to grow and expand their humanness.

I see this inability to let go of hurtful feelings and behaviors manifested in many ways. There is the mother who says, "My son is failing in school, and I am making him study for four hours a day. If that doesn't work, I'll make him study for eight hours a day." Or the father who says, "I've whipped my boy every time he misbehaves, and if he continues to ... (fail to come home, smoke pot, fail in school, and so on) I'm gonna really beat hell out of him." When you point out to them that what they have done to solve the problem hasn't worked, so it's hardly logical to do more of the same, they'll agree, but they insist that they're going to do it anyhow. Human beings, how wonderful and strange we are!

I think of Anna in her therapy when the purely self-destructive effects of the bitter harboring of her rage and resentment were clearly demonstrated to everybody, including Anna. Her reply was, "I don't give a damn if it kills me; they [her parents] are still bastards and that's still the way I feel about them." It is ironic that Anna's psychological salvation lay in her forgiving her parents for what she perceived as their failure to provide her with love and security, and she could not forgive them. And in her cling-

---

ing to her righteous hatred, she was condemning herself to misery and despair.

Our need to punish someone for our frustrations and disappointments appears to be preemptive in terms of psychological priorities. This need is fairly easily remedied when the hated or feared or frustrating person is available to us in some vulnerable way. But it's impossible when they are invulnerable, as parents are to a young child or when they are emotionally absent, as cold, aloof parents may be. It's especially damaging when they are physically absent and invulnerable, as are parents who divorce and leave or desert their families or die.

In the event that the objects of our frustrations are not available to us for direct retaliation, we are in trouble. The strong feelings arising from severe childhood disappointments cannot be ignored because they simply won't go away. They can be repressed and sometimes, in fortunate circumstances, they can be redirected in more productive ways. But often this cannot happen because of the strength of the feelings and because of the unfortunate turn of life's circumstances. Typically, they serve to fester and burn as life's stresses and problems and the demands of human growth occur. These rageful emotions will be directed at something and will be expressed in behavior. Unfortunately, such displaced expressions of poisonous feelings always fail as suitable outlets and discharges because they are not directed at the appropriate objects. We act ragefully toward friends and children and ourselves, which satisfies nothing.

In Anna's case, which is typical, she has incorporated her parents into her own personality. They own part of her. And, in her attempts to punish them, she punishes herself. In effect, she says to us, "I can't quit hurting because I must punish those who failed me, and they are in me, so I must suffer to insure that they suffer." How sweet vengeance

really is! When we look at self-destructive, disabling behavior and feelings in this light and realize that such persons are
not punishing themselves, but rather are flailing the souls of
someone who lives in their personality, then it makes sense
that we cling to our hurting. To quit hurting demands that
we forgive ourselves and the other hated people that live
within us.

I can hear the reader disclaim, "Surely you don't claim
this as a really consequential cause of emotional distress?"
I know I will get that response from the reader since I get
it from my colleagues when I try these ideas on them. At
first I tried to compromise on this formulation of my ideas
on what Freud calls resistance. "Well," I'd say, "certainly
incorporation accounts for a great deal of distress." But I
had difficulty in trying to account for the distress I saw in
others except in this way. So now I say, without blushing
or blanching: Incorporation and punishment of persons who
were looked to for psychological nourishment in early
childhood and who failed to fulfill these needs accounts for
almost all neurotic distress. And I believe it. Of course,
"normal" emotional distress may arise in a realistic way in
everyone's life when we suffer losses or accidents and illnesses or failures and sorrows.

You may argue that childish rages, fears, and disappointments do not carry much affective weight, that they are
transitory and are forgotten in the passage of time. But they
aren't forgotten. They will emerge sometime in life, and
they are not weak in an affective sense. If the four-year-old
child had the strength of an adult, no parent would survive.
They would literally die as a result of the rage of childish
disappointments. When I say "disappointment," I use the
term in its broader psychological sense to mean a failure to
provide a necessary psychological need. I don't refer to the
"disappointment" a child suffers when he doesn't get to go

outside and play or when his favorite toy is broken. I refer to the "disappointment" he suffers when he is threatened with the loss of love and care, or when he is charged with tasks that are beyond his capacity but whose satisfactory completions are necessary to earn continued parental care, protection, interest, concern, and love. His loss, or the threatened loss, of those essential psychological supplies causes anxiety, then frustration, then resentment, and finally rage.

This rage may be expressed in diverse ways. And I don't understand why it goes one way or the other. For instance, the rage engendered over parental failure to provide protection and care because of alcoholism may be manifested in a child's later life in a rigid abstinence from alcohol consumption and by a compulsive, obsessive personality in other life functions. Or it may result in rage turned to depression and finally to suicide. How this rage, engendered by disappointment, will emerge and what form it will take is anybody's guess in any given case. The only certainties are that it will emerge and that it will be attended to in some fashion.

The rage I speak of is a rage that demands retribution. It is a powerful, commanding emotion, and it will not be denied its expression in one way or the other. Direct vengeance is the most direct expression of this, but it is rarely available as an outlet. The power of this was expressed by Heinrich Heine (and repeated by Freud in *Civilization and Its Discontents*):

> Mine is the most peaceable disposition. My wishes are a humble dwelling with a thatched roof, but a good bed, good food, milk and butter of the freshest, flowers at the window, some fine tall trees before my door; and if the good God wants to make me completely happy, he will grant me the

joy of seeing some six or seven of my enemies hanging from these trees. With my heart full of deep emotion I shall forgive them before they die all the wrong they did in my lifetime. True, one must forgive one's enemies, but not until they are brought to execution.

To see yourself

I have tried to reveal myself in these pages. In some ways I am sure that I have; in many ways, I haven't. Perhaps what the reader sees as gaps, omissions, exaggerations, and pure fabrications will be more instructive to him than what I consciously meant to say.

I deliberately left out some material that may well have had some bearing on the issues I discussed. Most of the omissions, however, were made because I felt they were relatively unimportant, although I realize that I am probably the poorest judge possible of what is or isn't pertinent to this story. But, in this effort, I was the only judge available. I am keenly aware that there are blind spots in my self-perception. However, I don't believe that this places an impenetrable screen over the picture of my life. You may understand more than you would imagine by observing the areas of life's experience that were omitted or dealt with superficially.

I have resisted the impulse to dress up this account by manufacturing events and dramatizing issues or by obscuring my feelings and behavior. It would not be fair to the reader or to me to have done so. Because of this, you will observe some immature, juvenile, self-serving feelings and behavior. It is necessary to show you these things if I am going to serve anyone's needs by this account. I am sure that the reader is not interested in a narrative of another life "nobly led." The era of the romanticized life is over, and we are the better for it. Much of my life and yours is made up of self-serving, thoughtless, dishonorable, and cruel actions. I have tried to show myself in this regard openly and honestly. I am committed to the belief that my worth to myself and others is measured by my growing in qualities that make me more open and more useful to others. I simply have had a long way to go.

It is hard, almost impossible, to fully show yourself to others. Sidney Jourard, who wrote *The Transparent Self,* says that self-disclosure is necessary if we are to grow in our humanness. It's his conviction that neurosis and psychosis bed down in the secret recesses of our personality and that they can only be exorcised by the light of opening ourselves to others. I believe this to be essentially true, and, of course, my selfish purpose is served through these pages, for as I have opened myself to you, I have been able to free myself to some extent to grow in life's fullness. I find it dismaying to see how much further I need to go.

I know that I have managed to straighten my thoughts out about one important subject, freedom and commitment. I have found that life's taskmaster is an exacting, merciless, fair, but rigid accountant. He pays in the coin of equitable exchange. To experience great joy you are required to submit yourself to great pain, or at least the possibilities of such. Great gain demands great sacrifice. Absolute freedom is possible only through absolute commitment.

You can guard yourself against the possibilities of sorrow by loving no one deeply. But then you must give up the possibilities of the deep satisfaction of having someone who is committed to you. Limited involvement with others may protect you from the chance of pains inflicted on you by others' deaths, illnesses, disappointments, and betrayals. But you will pay for your protection in the unfulfilled life, in the life of pleasures that are bland because they are not shared, in the delight of achievement that is empty because no one cares, in the joy of giving to the growing ability of someone else to find meaning in his world because there is really no need for you to do so. This is the bargain we make for the full life: "I will accept responsibilities for someone else in order that I may share in his joy. I will bear his sorrow and suffer his pain to be with him in his wonder and delight. My freedom is gained in my commitment and my life is saved for me to live it when I find that I can give it up."

I am under no illusion that I have "made it" as an example of a man who has gained the full life. I am far from it. The only comfort I can lay any legitimate claim to is that I know what I must do, and I am trying to do it.

Coming back

I suppose that each of us feels that our troubles and our despair are unique and unparalleled. And in a sense they are. But in a more profound sense, we share our fate with others. This is especially true for those who have managed to make themselves a part of someone else and who have let someone else share their humanity. To truly savor joy, we must experience it with someone else. To make despair bearable, we must let others experience it with us. The only way we can transcend "quiet desperation" is to open ourselves to the possibility that someone else, if we let him, may come to be *with* us. If, however, we decide that the risk of sharing is greater than the joy, we are doomed to the ultimate despair of loneliness.

To share is to gain the strength to face openly and fully the fact that life has no meaning unless we give it meaning and to know that what happens to any one of us does in fact happen to all of us. Such sharing may make it possible to surrender our need for vengeance and our quest for domination and control. We may find that by helping others exercise their humanity, we can express and experience our own. But this doesn't come to us without pain or without struggle.

As long as we resist the experiencing of our feelings, good and bad, we can never call these feelings to task and require them to serve us. Rather we are doomed to struggle inconclusively, to evade and avoid the darker moments of our living, never knowing why we are so unhappy and miserable.

Let yourself hurt. Experience your grief and fear, surrender to frustration and humiliation. Know thyself. In knowing, we can be free. In *The Flies,* a play by Jean-Paul Sartre, Orestes says, "Human life begins on the far side of despair." Sorrow and disappointment can be used to reveal to us our way to peace and comfort, to gladness and joy, if we face them in the presence of someone who understands and cares. To submit to the possibility of failure and pain is to gain the opportunity for a deeper, fuller life. Anything less may truly doom us to lead our own "lives of quiet desperation."

Open or closed?

I have felt moments of openness, moments of being my "best self." But they are too rare and apparently too threatening, for I don't sustain them for long. Instead, I withdraw to a feeling of dull numbness. My demeanor (I hope I am reporting this fairly objectively) becomes cold, aloof, and rigid. I don't want to be that way. I can see people approaching me at those times in a hesitant, fearful way. I can see myself giving them formal politeness and correct responses but without any warmth or spontaneity. I know that they won't tell me much of themselves, their concerns, or their work. They cannot share themselves with me because obviously they can see that I can't reveal or share much of myself with them. I know they must think, "It would have to be hell to work near that guy, or live with him." And it is.

For those of you who have some interest in the clinical details, I can report that twelve years after my "despair," I am at work, primarily administrating a psychological services program and apparently doing a creditable job. In those years I have been unable to report to work on only two occasions. But don't let me mislead you. There are many days when I was deeply depressed, on the verge of being unable to even speak rationally when required. There have been many days when I was afraid that I could tolerate no more. But so far, I have tolerated. It distresses me that so much of my energy and ability has been consumed in this manner and that I haven't enjoyed living as I might have enjoyed it. I haven't experienced the warmth and joy of friendship and companionship that I might have, and I haven't been able to give of myself as I desperately want to, especially to those whom I hold dear, who need me and have borne my burden with me.

It distresses me that life, with increasing fleetness, is passing by and I am not living it to its fullest. I am sorry that only too rarely can I experience the freedom and joy of openness and of the sharing of myself.

A continuous search

As I read these words over now, I think, "Now there's a man who's depressed!" But I don't really believe that this is entirely the state of mind that these words reflect. I hope they reflect my concern that for me "the search for meaning" is just now underway. This search has to be made by each of us, for each of us. It can't be done for you by somebody else. Fortunately for some people the search is not too painful and the finding at the end is acceptable. For others, and it appears that this includes me, the way is full of thorns and brambles and the path is treacherous. At the considerable risk of being laboriously pedantic, I am trying to say that my personal efforts to make order and meaning of my own existence are tough. The lyrics of a song I heard the other day on my car radio went, "Life gets teejus, don't it?" And it does. Many of you probably know what I mean. For many of us are working at this task.

This search for meaning can culminate in individual rapture or despair. It can produce social consequences of the highest human value or the lowest animal degradation. Dickens and Mark Twain were searching for this meaning when they gave the world Tiny Tim and Huck Finn. Some of the most ennobling men and women of history have given the world meaning in their personal search for meaning. Without being presumptuous, we might include people like Christ, Schweitzer, and Eleanor Roosevelt and philosophers such as Tillich, Kierkegaard, Dewey, and Carl Rogers.

The search for meaning can culminate in personal and social tragedy, sometimes of a catastrophic scope. Witness the still unbelievable, incredible atrocities of Hitler as he searched for his meaning. Incidentally, we still have not fully and openly comprehended the scope and extent and the human implications of the overt manifestations of his (and his cohorts') grinding, spewing hate. Perhaps it is part of our psychological protection that we cannot.

A young man named Whitman was engaged in a cataclysmic struggle for meaning in his life when he mounted a tower at the University of Texas and shot people at random. His inability to find any acceptable way to approach the struggle for meaning may have finally led to this final virulent discharge of his anguish. (The tumor in his brain may be wholly responsible. I am sometimes haunted by the thought that all of these painful spiritual and emotional gyrations I feel in searching, wondering, hoping, may be as meaningless as the drift of smoke with the wind. Suppose this turmoil simply results from the wrong amount of hormones or brain chemicals or a brain with severely aberrant circuitry? What a terrible, yet appealing, thought!)

The point of all this, if I have a point, is that regardless of any other circumstances, we each must make the search. If we find it easily, well and good. Those people who do seem to make up the bulk of the earth's population. But if the struggle is long and hard, one of two consequences is possible, either great accomplishment (personal or social or both) or great despair and destruction (personal or social or both). Of course, for some who struggle, the culmination never comes. On their last day they are still engaged in the task. But perhaps this is the only possible solution to some problems—that we must continuously struggle with them.

What then will it be for me? What will it be for you? Perhaps some of you who read this will decide that the struggle is no longer tolerable and give up, either your physical life or perhaps "only" your emotional existence. But it is my hope that you may now be renewed by the knowledge and the reassurance that the struggle has been won, and won magnificently, by some who have fought just as you and I are now engaged.

Your anguish and mine are not ours alone. They are shared in some measure by all men. If this were not so, it would be as Camus says: "Life as a human being is absurd." But it is not absurd because we are a part of each other. And when we are part of another we share his joy and we bear a portion of his sadness, and even his emotional or physical demise must, to fulfill our own humanness, be ours to a degree. This is the way we must struggle to come to be. John Donne recognized this when he said, "Any man's death diminishes me because I am involved in mankind."

The human world is not a bestial jungle. Most people want to be a part of those they love. If you don't believe it, just ask. The kindness, sympathy, understanding, and support of most people is ours for the asking—if we could just ask for it.

Dying does get tiresome

12

I<small>T SEEMED</small> that I had been in psychotherapy all my adult life. In fact, I had been for a considerable portion of it. Four years of individual therapy with Carl and nearly two years of group therapy and still I was slipping perceptibly downhill. I was in real despair over my apparent failure to become more competent in managing my life and my happiness. The repetitive, tiresome pendulum of depression and anxiety swung back and forth in my life, pausing only briefly at the point of balance. It ground me down bit by bit until I felt I could stand it no longer.

I had tried all Saturday morning to reach Carl. I called his office, his home, and his answering service. But I couldn't find him. I was in a state of near collapse. I had slept little for three nights with continual panic attacks alternating with agitated periods of depression. My wife had taken the children and left the house. She knew, and I knew, that I couldn't maintain my composure in front of them. More and more often over the past few months I had been forced to retreat to my bedroom and lock the door. I'd stay there for hours, sometimes doing nothing, but often crying and cursing myself and my fate. Sometimes, without warning, the depressive episodes would suddenly lift and I would feel pretty good. My mood swings were so wide that they frightened me and left my wife in a continuous state of turmoil.

Sometimes I would leave the house for work feeling pretty good and chipper. But an hour later at the office I would feel so terrible and have so little control over myself that I couldn't even carry on a lucid conversation. At those times I would ask my secretary to take my calls and to tell visitors that I was out. However, an hour or so later, I would be able to return my calls and take care of the ordinary affairs of the day. It got to be like an unpredictable, horrible roller coaster ride.

Somehow the weekends were always worst. Saturday was bad, but Sunday was horrible. I would wake up, usually in a start, and feel so restless and anxious that I'd have to get up even when I hadn't slept enough. Still I felt pretty fair. After two or three cups of coffee and a doughnut or two, I'd begin to feel shaky and anxious, and my guts would tremble. Along about ten or eleven o'clock in the morning, I'd feel so uptight and so driven that I would be frantic. It didn't happen every weekend, but over the past few months it had become more frequent and more intense. Somehow weekdays weren't usually quite so bad. Naturally, I thought it must be because I had nothing to do on the weekends. Perhaps the fact that I had to work Monday through Friday helped to keep me together and functioning on those days, I thought.

But, for whatever reasons, things were getting tougher for me. I had almost lost the ability to sleep through the night. Sometimes I couldn't go to sleep at all. Other times I would awaken and be unable to go back to sleep. I was bone-tired all the time. In the morning I would get up and shave and bathe. Then I would have to sit down for a few minutes and rest before I could start to dress. After I dressed, I would rest for a minute or two before drinking a cup of coffee and perhaps eating toast or cereal. Then I'd get into my car and drive to the office. On the way to the office I'd think about the fact that I was going to have to leave my car in the parking lot and walk to my office. This was a trip of two short blocks. I actually dreaded it. After I parked my car I'd sit there for five minutes or so waiting to gather enough energy to make it to my desk.

Increasing panic

I had more frequent attacks of agitated panic culminating in feelings of impending death and in near unconsciousness. These attacks were unpredictable and seemingly unrelated to what was going on around me. They could happen in periods of stress or while I was having fun at a party. They happened at work when I was alone or at a meeting when I was with other people. I wracked my brain to try to understand what dynamic significance these attacks must have. I worked at trying to penetrate my unconscious and to ferret out the terrible things that must be going on there. I really almost drove myself crazy analyzing every event and all the people around me, belaboring my feelings, motives, and thoughts until I trusted no one, especially myself.

The attacks were not only coming more frequently, but they were more violent, lasted longer, and depleted me for two or three days afterward. Up until the last few weeks these episodes were marked by generalized anxiety, fatigue, and feelings of depression and lethargy. But now the attacks were getting a little more difficult to manage.

I was in the building library one morning looking for a reference book I needed. As I went through some book titles in the stacks, I was suddenly aware that I was feeling quite anxious and tense. As I continued I could feel my stomach "quivering." I felt cold and shaky, but sweat broke out on my face. By the time I got back to the office my legs were so weak they could hardly carry me, and I was staggering from a disturbance of equilibrium.

As I plopped down in my chair I thought to myself, "You're the craziest son of a bitch that ever lived. Looking through a stack of books causes you to go into a state of agitated panic. A bastard as crazy as you ought to be dead." By now, of course, I was talking to myself as if I were really someone else. My agitation increased. I began to hyperventilate, and I broke out in a cold sweat all over my body. I felt like I was going to die. I was gasping for breath, thinking that I was going to lose consciousness any minute. I was in a devastating panic of fear. I was so weak that I couldn't get up from my chair. So I sat there in fear and trembling, feeling as if I would die at any moment.

This lasted about thirty minutes. But it left me so debilitated and depleted that I felt weak and sick for two or three days afterward.

My feelings now fell within a narrow range. I felt like hell all of the time, or worse. The episodes were more clearly defined now; rather than being vague and chronic, they were acute and pronounced. If they occurred when I was in a group, I would leave and try to get home or at least to my office, where I could hide out for the onslaught. If I was in a car driving, I would have to pull over and park. Then I would lie down on the front seat, almost in a stupor, until the attack passed and I could drive again.

Even between attacks I was functioning only marginally. I had a chronic, mild headache that was always worse in the morning. I was always weak and tired, but the symptom that bothered me the most was the disturbance in my equilibrium and balance. When I stood up I would pause for a moment with my hand on something to steady myself until I could get my bearings and start moving. Often in walking I would stagger or trip. My friends would joke, "What's R. drinking today?"

I had learned through sad experience that alcohol was devastating for me. If I had a few drinks when I was tired and tense, I would soon have a bonafide depressive condition. And hangovers were real dillies! Even after only a few drinks at a party, I would wake at two or three in the morning with a pounding headache and a stomach that felt as if it were going to crawl out of my throat. So I had learned over the past year or so that I simply couldn't drink liquor. And I seldom did.

So, see a doctor

As I look over what I have written, I can see the reader saying, "Why didn't you see a physician? Something was physically wrong." Well, I did. I saw several doctors. I complained of chronic headache, sleeplessness, anxiety, panic attacks, giving each one a long list of symptoms to consider. And they all thought, just as I did, that these symptoms were related to depression or depressive equivalents. Several recommended shock treatments. I even tried to convince my psychotherapist, Carl, that the only thing left for me to try was shock treatments. He resisted the idea, thinking that even if I got relief, it would only permit me to avoid dealing with those conflicts in my life that were causing my troubles.

But he was perplexed too. "I really don't understand," he said to me once. "You have made excellent progress in your psychotherapy. You should be functioning more effectively, more freely." He sent me to see a physician too.

During these months and years I probably had every kind of medicine prescribed for me that is available for psychotropic purposes. I took Tofranil, an antidepressant; Mellaril, a tranquilizer; Librium, a tranquilizer; and Sinequan, an antidepressant and tranquilizer. At one time or another, I was tried on virtually every psychotropic medication, especially tranquilizers and antidepressants, that was available. The only one of all I took that seemed to have any effect in the least was Dexamyl. This is an amphetamine preparation with a little sedative in it. In other words, a "pep pill." At times a Dexamyl would pull me out of an incapacitating depressive-panic episode in a matter of minutes. However, it didn't last long. I was sorely tempted many times to take them more often than prescribed. But I never exceeded the prescribed dosage. The rest of the medication appeared to be of no help whatsoever.

In spite of any medication and regardless of the fact that my psychotherapy was going well, I was getting worse. In a sense, the old saw, "The operation was a success, but the patient died," applied in my case.

The last of the last straws

Finally that Saturday morning Carl returned my call. He listened patiently to my reiteration (for he had heard it many times before from me) of my condition and my desperation. "Well, R.," he said, "I don't know what else you can do if you can't go on. I can put you in a hospital; we can try shock treatment." I protested, "But I don't want to do that." I went on, "Let me try a course of Tofranil again. It's been several years since I tried it." Carl sighed audibly on the phone, "All right, R., I'll call in a prescription for it." So once again I tried medicine, and once again, there were no appreciable results.

After my frantic call to Carl, two events occurred, several months apart, that finally resulted in the action that was to change the course of my life. Both were critical, but I didn't perceive their full significance at the time.

My wife and I were invited to a party at a hunting lodge in the country. We got there about six o'clock in the evening. We met some old friends and were introduced to some new ones. We both accepted a drink; mine was bourbon and water. We talked, told jokes, danced, and listened to music awhile. By 9:30 I was ravenously hungry, but dinner wasn't ready. I remember mixing a fourth drink and thinking that I'd better not have another without some food. That's the last thing I remember until sometime the next day. The rest of the party, coming back home, and going to bed were not in my memory. I woke up about 10 A.M. with the familiar pounding in my head and trembling in my stomach. It took awhile before it dawned on me that I had no recollection of anything after mixing that fourth drink at the party. I was informed by my wife that I had really made an ass of myself during the course of the evening. I asked her to spare me the details. I was profoundly shaken. I had walked, talked, and otherwise behaved in some fashion for twelve hours, and I had no remembrance of any of it. I was perplexed and frightened, and I seldom had a drink of any alcoholic beverage after that.

The second event also helped me to see the possible significance of physical facts affecting my behavior.

I had awakened one morning about 2:30. These early morning interruptions of my sleep were becoming commonplace, occurring once or twice a week. With a start my eyes jumped open and I lay there in the dark with the old familiar feeling of trembling in my guts and panic in my mind. As usual, I began hyperventilating and sweating. I got out of bed prepared to tough it out as I usually did until the episode was over. However, the curious thing to me is that even though I was thoroughly familiar with all the symptoms and the course of these attacks, I was still panic-stricken each time. Each time I felt impending death. Each time I was wild with despair and frustration.

I got up and went to the kitchen ready to pace the floor, as I usually did, alternating between cursing and moaning and otherwise acting like a wounded animal. I was thirsty, and as I started to get a drink of water from the faucet, I saw a pitcher of orange juice that had been left on the counter. I don't really care much for juice, but for some reason I poured with trembling hands a full glass of juice and drank it. I resumed my pacing and ruminating.

"It's in my imagination," I said to myself, "or is my stomach really calming down?" During these times, my guts felt like they were crawling around in my belly. In another minute or two I could feel my bodily musculature relaxing. I sat down. Soon my headache was gone and I felt calmer and easier than I had for months. "Well, I'll be damned," I said to myself again. "I am as relaxed and comfortable as if I had been shot full of some sedatives. Could a little sugar in orange juice do that?" I was truly astounded and perplexed. I had the first feeble thought that perhaps, just maybe, I wasn't totally crazy. It might just be possible that I had physical problems as well as emotional ones.

I treated the next attack with sugar. Two days later at work I felt weak and trembly and anxious. I got a Coke and some cookies. Sure enough, in a few minutes I was okay again. I had known for a long time that if I could eat a big meal, I would feel better. But sometimes I was so sick I couldn't eat. For several months prior to my discovery, or realization, of the role of sugar in my feelings, I had been eating candy like a starved five-year-old. I kept hard candy on my desk and ate as much as a half pound of it in a day.

Any number of times I would eat a pound of peanut brittle or a quart of ice cream at one sitting. I stopped some of that when I nearly lost all my teeth from decay.

I satisfied myself through repeated trials over the next few weeks that sugar was doing something to me. What, I didn't know. But what to do about it? As soon as I go to a physician and he finds out my history of emotional problems, he'll prescribe another tranquilizer and that will be it.

Another diagnosis

Then it occurred to me that I should try my family physician, the man who treats our colds, sore throats, and pulled muscles. I made an appointment and went to see him. I reviewed my history of emotional problems and told him of my discovery of the effect that food, especially sugar, had on me. I asked him to please examine me physically and ignore psychological factors. He agreed and drew some blood for tests.

"Your blood sugar is 65," he said. "And that's somewhat low. Come back on Wednesday and we'll run a glucose tolerance test to see if you are having a metabolic problem."

On Wednesday I went back to his office, having skipped breakfast according to his instructions. I drank a bottle of flavored sugar water at 9 A.M. and sat down to read a magazine. The technician took blood samples periodically. At 9:30 I felt fine. At 10 o'clock everything was okay. By 10:30 I was feeling a bit shaky, and by 11 o'clock I was so sick I could hardly sit up.

I went back the next day to see the doctor for the results. "Well!" he said thoughtfully, looking at the folder on his desk, "you really can't handle sugar. Your count was down to 40 two hours after you took the glucose." He explained that a normal blood sugar ranges from 80 to 110. He looked at me and said, "I'll bet you felt like hell, didn't you?" I just nodded, really too stunned to talk. He continued, "I don't see how you've kept going. Come back in a week and let's repeat the test to be certain."

The test a week later showed the same results. I was in a state of turmoil. Was it possible that at least some part of my trouble was physically rather than psychologically caused? I was fearful, yet hopeful, for I had had my hopes crushed too many times before by expectations about drugs that didn't work, or by spurious feelings of short-lived episodes of well-being. I was cautious, but I felt in my gut there was hope.

"I think I'd better send you to Dr. H., a specialist in metabolic disorders," Dr. B. said. "What do I do in the meantime?" I asked. "Well," he replied thoughtfully, "you need to keep your sugar level up. Why don't you eat or drink something sweet about every two hours."

It so happens that my condition, reactive hypoglycemia, is badly aggravated by sugar. A rapid infusion of sugar in the blood stimulates the pancreas to release insulin, which is necessary in metabolizing sugar. However, in reactive hypoglycemia, the pancreas over-reacts to sugar and releases too much insulin, depleting the blood sugar and dropping it to dangerously low levels. When that happens, as I later discovered, the brain is deprived of its only fuel, sugar, and myriad symptoms such as weakness, dizziness, anxiety, sweating, hunger, or even nausea can occur. Of course, if the sugar level continues to drop, coma and even death can ensue. But this never happens in reactive hypoglycemia because the body responds to this emergency with adrenalin, which causes the liver to release additional sugar into the blood and which, incidentally, may cause anxiety, hyperventilation, palpitations, and feelings of impending death.

So you can see, as I can now, that by taking sugar every

two hours, I was in the same predicament as the fireman who was spraying a burning house with gasoline. The more sugar I took, the more intense the symptoms became.

After about a day and a half of eating or drinking some sugar every two hours, I was nearly a basket case. "My God, I can't continue with this: I'll die or go completely nuts," I told my wife. I was shaking and quivering and stammering by then. "I'll quit the sugar bit entirely." Of course, that turned out to be a fortunate decision. My symptoms subsided and I made it to the endocrinologist. By taking such large quantities of sugar I was causing an excessive outpouring of insulin by the pancreas, which in turn was rapidly depleting the glucose level in my blood. The body responds to this emergency with an outpouring of epinephrine, which stimulates the release of stored supplies of sugar in the liver. However, epinephrine is a powerful stimulant. "A characteristic pattern in hypoglycemia is tachycardia, anxiety, sweating, pallor, and rise of blood pressure," according to Beeson and McDermott in the *Textbook of Medicine.*

A change of direction

The exhaustive tests that followed added no really new information to the diagnosis. I had a common form of reactive hypoglycemia with no signs of a tumor or other agent that was causing it. My problem was not entirely physical by any means. I am certain that years of stress, anxiety, fearfulness, and bitter resentment caused my body to have to operate under emergency conditions much of the time. It's not difficult to see that this could result in a disturbed metabolism. But one certainly contributed to the other. The devastation done to my psychological functioning by the hypoglycemic episodes was profound. In *Body, Mind, and Sugar,* Dr. S. A. Portis is quoted as describing the symptoms of low blood sugar to include chronic fatigue, "acute attacks of extreme weakness, tremulousness, sweating, and vertigo. At times a feeling of lightheadedness may be manifest. The acute attacks may be associated with anxiety of fainting or free floating anxiety." Abrahamson and Pezet go on to say, "We recognize these symptoms as being typical of the milder forms of functional hyperinsulinism."

I had become convinced that I was a hopeless nut, that I would never master my own destiny. I was certain that my unconscious was thick with entangled and ensnarled hostilities and frustrations. I had no trust in myself and no confidence in what tomorrow might bring. I never knew when I might break down or finally crack up and have to be "put away."

I was continually afraid that I would give up and destroy myself in utter despair. I was afraid to really be with other people for fear they would see my misery and anxiety. My speech was a dead giveaway. At times I could hardly talk. My mind could not coordinate my thinking with my tongue. I stuttered and stammered. I developed the habit of long pauses in responding to someone in order to give myself time to think about how I would respond and how I would get my mouth to say what I wanted it to say. It was a long time before I could be persuaded that such severe symptoms could result from something as innocuous sounding as "low blood sugar." However, in the thirteenth edition of the *Textbook of Medicine* by Beeson and McDermott, hypoglycemia symptoms are described fully. They "may take the form of confusion, hallucinations, aimless hyperactivity, or even convulsions." The only positive thing I can think of that came out of my experience of hypoglycemia is that I learned how much I can take if I have to, and I learned what misery some people have endured. I hope it has contributed to my ability to be compassionate toward the suffering of others and to understand their behavior. For these things I am thankful, but I wish I could have learned them an easier way.

The diagnostic work at the hospital confirmed the diagnosis. The treatment was simple. I could take no sugar at all and had to strictly limit my intake of other carbohydrates. In effect, this meant I had to follow a high protein diet. Also, I could not drink alcoholic beverages. What a small price to pay for a new life! Within just a few days I began to feel better. However, all was not clear sailing; I still had occasional hypoglycemic attacks even on the diet. But they were fewer and less severe. Also, I reacted to them less emotionally. Since I knew what was happening, it was much less frightening. As the weeks and months went by the attacks subsided and I began to feel normal again. I was able to start a day with a relative certainty that I would finish it feeling about as I did when I started it. I began to sleep all night and to wake up refreshed and able to look forward to the day.

I stopped all medication when the hypoglycemia was diagnosed. After nearly three years, I have not taken a single tranquilizer, antidepressant, or stimulant, and I have not needed to. My condition has stabilized to what Freud called "normal unhappiness." The problems of work and life and living are just as great for me as they are for anyone else. But no greater.

It took over a year of steady and conscientious dieting before I no longer was subject to unexpected swings of mood or attacks of fatigue and depression. After that year, I discontinued psychotherapy and have not needed to return for help.

The sun shines brighter and the days are sweeter. My work is mostly a challenge rather than a chore, and my energy is available for me to use rather than consumed in merely living. The dread for what the future might bring and the dismal despair I felt about the rest of my life are in the past. I can love those I love more freely and subject them to less of my frustration and anger.

I look back on those days with wonder and not with bitterness. I feel like a condemned criminal who has been unexpectedly pardoned. I am too thankful to be fully alive to indulge myself in regret. It's almost as if I have had two lifetimes. One filled with anger, despair, and fear and one with pleasure, accomplishment, and happiness. I know that I have been given a chance to use my life and now I have a brand new but more pleasant problem. How will I use it?

Hypoglycemia explained

"Hypoglycemia exists when the blood glucose concentration falls below 50 mg. per 100 ml.," according to Beeson and McDermott. Hypoglycemia, or low blood sugar, can be caused by a number of things. In the diabetic who is taking insulin it may be caused by too much insulin with too little food, causing a precipitous drop in blood sugar. It can be the result of a tumor in the pancreas causing the islets to release an oversupply of insulin in the blood, dropping sugar levels. There are also other disease processes which can result in hypoglycemia. However, the most common cause of hypoglycemic episodes is the reactive variety. Some authorities, such as Marble and associates, feel that hypoglycemia is a result of rather than a cause of emotional stress and psychological problems. In *Diabetes Mellitus* Joslin says, "Since it is often associated with anxiety or emotional upsets, it is sometimes difficult to separate symptoms due to hypoglycemia from those related to anxiety; in fact, there is some discussion as to whether this type of hypoglycemia is the result of rather than the cause of anxiety." Whatever causes it, however, chronic hypoglycemia or repeated acute attacks can lead to grave emotional and psychological complications.

Prolonged and chronic hypoglycemia can lead to cerebral damage. When blood sugar drops to frank hypoglycemic levels, gross and fine neurological disturbances can occur. Contrary to the generally accepted belief that episodes of hypoglycemia are brief and only transitory when blood sugar levels are corrected, I can testify to the fact that the debilitating effects of a single episode can last for several hours or even days when the attack has been especially severe or prolonged. Raising blood sugar levels does alleviate the acute and most distressing symptoms, but the effect on body and mind can persist in a most distressing fashion for some time afterward.

The symptoms associated with hypoglycemia are so varied, confusing, and often so subtle that persons suffering from the condition have been diagnosed and treated for every imaginable ailment. Abrahamson and Pezet say, "Persons who at last were found to be suffering from hyperinsulinism have been treated for coronary thrombosis and other heart ailments, brain tumors, epilepsy, gall bladder disease, appendicitis, and every sort of neurosis. They have been told repeatedly that their trouble is 'all in the mind' and sent to the psychoanalyst."

It is also easy to see that the disorder may develop quite slowly and persist in its course over a long period of time. In fact, someone suffering from hypoglycemia may become so accustomed to his symptoms that for him life itself is just a long series of fatiguing events interspersed with attacks of collapse and exhaustion. Often such persons are dismissed with the casual description of "constitutionally frail" or "hysterical exhaustion." Finally some crisis, or even an unrelated illness, may reveal the fact that some of these persons have a "real" reason to feel as they do. The gradual onset of the condition is certainly the major reason for this. Abrahamson and Pezet also say, "The malady develops insidiously. At first there is an occasional slight feeling of lightheadedness. Then, in the course of a few years, perhaps, the frequency and severity of the attacks increase markedly, and the patient is assailed by ravenous hunger and utter fatigue. Soon other strange and disquieting symptoms creep up on him."

What is the contribution of the emotional life to this physically debilitating condition? The question can be complex if one considers every possible case and the intricate circumstances of each life affected by it. But they all seem to have a common denominator: namely, a disquieting lack of inner peace and comfort. Invariably, sufferers are hard driving, hard worrying, fear-driven, or hopeless people. The one thing they all lack is peace of mind. They are not in tune with themselves or their world. They harbor hate, resentment, and destructive aggression. They are afraid in a world which seems cold and heartless. They often see no possibility of safety, security, and warmth. They perceive their own heart dimly and insist that what is in their soul must be in yours and mine, and they are afraid.

I can see clearly now that my initial attacks of anxiety and depression were related to hypoglycemic episodes. These instances led eventually to my hospitalization for depression. I cannot honestly claim that these attacks were the cause of my depression and that I would have been spared my subsequent suffering if it had been detected and treated at that time. But I do wonder what course my life might have taken if it had.

Becoming a
psychologist

13

ADMINISTERING A PROGRAM of psychological services for handicapped children is my major job responsibility. I enjoy this
work and feel productive and useful in it. But I use more of
what I have learned in those years I have described in the
limited amount of clinical psychological work I do with
children and their parents. Confronting one person who
needs help calls for the exercise of all the clinical experience
and training I can muster. The skills and knowledge one
may get in a graduate program help. But the real development of competency depends on the practice of these skills
with people in distress. This chapter, then, illustrates how
I have taken what I learned in graduate school and in my
personal therapy and applied it to how I live and work and
think now.

Apparently, there is a first time for everything. Certainly
there is a first time that an airline pilot lands a plane full of
passengers. There is a first time for the surgeon to assume
responsibility for a patient's operation. Somewhere, somehow, there was a first time for every chef who ever prepared
a meal. And there was a time for every practicing psycholo-

gist when the person facing him was his initial and his final responsibility.

Although chefs, surgeons, pilots, and psychologists undergo relatively lengthy periods of training and preparation, and even though they perform repeatedly under supervision the tasks that they will later undertake independently, still there comes that fateful day when the responsibility is not shared and the benevolent, helpful observers are gone. This initial assumption of independent responsibility is a lonely and frightening moment. I feel confident too that the delivery of services at that time is not as effective and as useful as it will come to be when sound competency replaces abject fear in the practitioner.

Those initial efforts must surely result in some rough landings for airplane travelers, some poor meals for diners, perhaps fatal consequences for a few surgical patients, and certainly, some bemused and confused clients of psychologists.

My problems in getting myself successfully through this period of developing professional competency were greatly compounded by my attempts to cope with the development and maintenance of my personal self. In many respects, these complementary tasks are necessarily a part of a compounded growth problem for everyone. However, my attempts to avert disaster in my personal development were more unusual and difficult than such problems generally are for the novice psychologist.

Practicing to practice

As most psychologists in training do, I spent a great deal of time in the guidance center administering various psychological tests, reading case notes, conducting exploratory and background interviews with clients and performing various other tasks of a semiprofessional and clerical nature. I observed others at work via the facility of the one-way mirror, the video tapes, and the ubiquitous tape recorder. We reviewed our work in the medium of seminars and through training sessions with an experienced supervisor. We assisted in therapeutic work with certain members of the clients' families, sought resources as needed, called consulting agencies, developed histories, and engaged in many other tasks that brought us into meaningful therapeutic contact with clients seeking help. We observed, experienced, and shared responsibility; and we learned and grew in competency, skill, and understanding. We began to feel useful and knowledgeable and to see how things that were perplexing could be made understandable and how the individual struggle for living could be made fruitful. I know we grew in professional skill and competency, and we felt competent. That is, we felt competent until the appointed day when we were handed the chart of someone and told that this was "our" client. "Come to us if you need any help. Otherwise you are on your own," the director of the center said to me one day.

Who needs help?

I looked at the folder in my hands as if it were the signed warrant for my execution. I opened it and a name floated into clear perception. I went through the material in the folder. "Oh God," I implored, "please don't let him have any bad problems." "Perhaps he is undecided about his choice of a major in college," I thought hopefully. "Surely they wouldn't give me a case that was serious." But I really knew that there isn't any other kind.

Bill Blank, my client, had a chronic intractable dermatosis. That sounded sufficiently serious to me. I read further.

He had skin eruptions on both arms extending from his elbows to his hands. "What the hell am I going to do about him," I thought miserably, "if medical science has failed to cure him?"

So the day of my first interview with Bill unavoidably came. "Maybe he won't come," I thought hopefully as I sat in my office rehearsing my opening words and gestures. "Hello, Mr. Blank, how are you?" I rejected that opening: "I can't ask a sick man how he's doing." How about this, "Sit down, Mr. Blank," and follow this by expectant silence, as I had been taught. "Hell," I thought, "I can't do that, I've got to say something. Suppose he just sits there and looks at me."

As the hour grew near I became more miserable, but I continued to hope that he wouldn't show up at all. But he did. The buzzer buzzed and the receptionist informed me that Mr. Blank had arrived. "Send him in," I replied.

I opened the door at his knock. We stood there in a frozen silence. Finally he spoke, "Hi, I'm Bill Blank." I managed to introduce myself and again we stood there looking at each other. At last I mustered a little self-control and invited him to sit down. "Where?" he asked. "Oh, anywhere you wish," I breezily replied. He headed for "my" chair at the same time I did. We bumped into each other and backed off, apologizing simultaneously. Warily he circled around me and safely got seated. With a convulsive sigh of relief I made it to my desk.

I don't remember those first few words. My senses and my thoughts were dazed. All I could think of consciously was how badly I needed to go to the bathroom. In my preoccupation with my anxiety prior to the interview I had repressed the urge to seek relief for an overextended bladder. Now I could no longer ignore it. I was miserable. "But,"

I thought, "I can't get up now. He'll think I'm crazy, if he doesn't already."

Between my overwhelming anxiety and my desperate need to obey nature's call, I must have said something, and he must have said something. But I will never remember just what.

Heal thyself

I was fortunate in being able to experience with my first client the resilience and potential for growth that most people have within them. Bill taught me that my job is to help and it's the client's job to do the work of change. In just a few sessions he told me what the problem was and how it could be solved.

Bill's father was a successful, aggressive lawyer who had decided that Bill would also study the law and practice with him after graduation. There were several problems with that particular plan, which Bill cleared up for me in a few weeks. The first difficulty was that Bill didn't really want to be a lawyer, he wanted to be a high school athletic coach. The second problem involved Bill's inability to compete with his highly aggressive father. He couldn't. He could never afford to do something as well as his father, because his father couldn't take it. Dad had quit playing golf when Bill began to beat him consistently. Dad claimed the press of business made it necessary to cut out golf.

The other major obstacle was that Bill was not as academically astute as his father. His scholastic potential for law school was poor. On the other hand, he compared fairly well with our university's physical education majors. Value judgments are not necessary for the recognition that lawyers, by and large, are sharper scholars than coaches are.

I am sure that coaches have unmeasured human qualities that are equally positive. But other qualities aside, Bill couldn't make it in law school. And his arms were covered with a suppurating rash that almost incapacitated him.

The problem seemed clear enough as Bill outlined it. He couldn't cut it in law school, and he didn't want to be a lawyer. He also suggested the solution—a transfer to the school of physical education. That sounded like an excellent plan to me. So my job, as I saw it, was to help Bill find acceptable reasons for himself and his dad to make this change in his life's direction. And I did. Bill transferred to the physical education department. He and his father started playing golf together again, and his arms were soon without a blemish. I wish all clients could be as successful.

Mistakes too

Success contributes to the development and extension of the psychologist's skills. So do mistakes and failures. It's ironic that sometimes our failures are better learning experiences than our successes. However, poor decisions and distressful outcomes are instructive only when we know about them and only when we are able to admit them and learn from them. Some psychologists go on year after year leaving a trail of confused, unsatisfied clients in their wake, excusing their failures by rationalizing that the client was "unmotivated" or "unwilling" to be helped. Sadder still are the unhappy people who leave our offices, no better off than when they came, because the psychologist says they are "better" or "well" or that "I've done all I can do for you. Now it's up to you." These psychologists are never taught by their failures because they have never had any!

I've had many instructive failures to learn from. Sometimes all that I've learned is to be able to predict more accurately how I will probably fail with a particular kind of client. I'm not too comfortable with this kind of learning, except that it's taught me to appreciate the fact that I don't know everything about my client even after a long period of time with him. I've also learned that a helpful interaction between me and another person depends to a large measure on our sharing information, feelings, and ideas. I used to believe that I should hold the power of secret knowledge (knowledge about my client, his strengths and weaknesses, his conflicts and problems) and that I could use this knowledge to "move" the client in the direction he "should" go. It won't work that way. I can't know everything, and I can't choose for someone else.

Eloise made a believer out of me. She was a tall, gaunt, unattractive college junior. Long and lanky, she reminded me of a crane on the marsh. Arms and legs intertwined, she would sit in my office looking uncomfortable. Her problem, she said, was anxiety, or as she put it, "I'm scared as hell."

"About what?" I asked. "Everything," she replied aggressively. "I'm afraid when I have to talk to people or give a report in class. I'm terrified when I go out with a guy. When I talk on the phone I stutter and stammer. I hate to even go out of my room."

We continued on this course for several weeks. I was concerned about Eloise. She was afraid. Always afraid. Her thoughts and feelings took the form of flights of fancy which were only loosely connected with what we were talking about. At times, I felt she forgot where she was and who I was. Her fantasies and feelings grew in succeeding weeks to be wilder and more farfetched. Underlying it all was the pervasive grip of anxiety and fear which ruled her life, a fear which I felt was forcing her to abandon the here and now for the more pleasant reality of her dreams.

But I didn't share my feelings and concerns with Eloise.

I didn't tell her how I felt about what she was saying and doing. Instead I tried to reinforce whatever attempts she was making to deal with "reality" as I saw reality. My efforts along this line seemed to be less and less useful. Often, she simply ignored me in a rather bizarre attempt to be alone in my presence. Naturally, as the possessor of secret knowledge, I shared none of this with her.

In the course of one session, when she was talking about her fears, I asked her how she spent her weekends. She sighed, "Usually by myself reading or at a movie or studying. About every other weekend I fly to New York for a modeling job I have with an agency there." I didn't hear the rest of her remarks. I was stunned. "The kid is delusional," I thought. "She really is out of it." I looked at her again. To my masculine eye she was downright homely, all legs and arms with just enough meat on her bones to keep them from punching holes in her skin.

"Poor thing," I thought. "Now she's imagining herself to be a beautiful, graceful woman. So attractive that people pay money to look at her."

"Tell me about these trips to New York," I cleverly requested. "What do you do? Whom do you work with? Tell me about it." She described her delusional modeling job in great detail, right down to the amount of money she was making.

"You're really doing all right in your dreams," I thought. "I'd better contact her parents or at least call the university health service. It may be necessary to hospitalize her."

I talked with one of the senior staff members, describing my problem with Eloise and her break from reality, as I saw it. Dr. T. agreed that it sounded to her like the poor girl had slipped into a psychotic delusion.

"What other evidences has she shown of delusional thinking?" Dr. T. asked. I detailed some of my feelings about Eloise and described her autistic withdrawal from me and how she seemed to be departing further and further from the real world as we know it.

This conversation finally convinced me that at our next appointment I would have to tell Eloise that I was going to call her parents and that we would have to find a more "secure" environment for her. I dreaded it.

Whose reality?

"I wish you could help me understand this," said Eloise at our next meeting, handing me some papers in a manila envelope. I opened it and took out a bundle of papers stapled together. It was a contract with a modeling agency, address New York City, New York, in Eloise's name! I was stunned. I looked at Eloise with a catastrophically altered perspective. I saw a frightened, lonely, unhappy girl who was not crazy at all and who had no notion that I thought she was.

I still had time to redeem myself. I could still say, "Eloise, I thought you were nuts. I thought you had dreamed up all this stuff about a modeling job in New York. My God, I'm so glad you aren't delusional, and I'm so appalled that I failed to tell you my thoughts and feelings." That's what I could have said. But I didn't. I looked up at her calmly and said quietly, "What is it that you don't understand about this, Eloise?"

I had a chance to make a move toward growth for myself and help for the girl, and I blew it. She left school at the end of the year just as lonely, just as confused, and just as unhappy as she was when I first saw her.

Another lesson learned

I kept seeing these anxious, uptight, fearful kids brought to me by perfectly reasonable, rational, pleasant mammas and daddies. I take a history—early development, diseases, accidents, traits and behaviors, school performance, likes and dislikes, presenting problems and concerns. I keep hearing the same story. "No significant developmental problems. Sue walked at ten months and said her first sentence at sixteen months. She was toilet-trained at two and has no bowel or bladder problems now."

"But she won't do her school work," her mother protests. "She cries without provocation and has temper tantrums if she doesn't have her way. If I leave the house for a few minutes and she can't find me, she has hysterics. She won't even let me shut the door to the bathroom because she says she is afraid she can't see me. I don't know what I'm going to do. Now, I can hardly get her to go to school. She cries every morning and complains that her stomach hurts. Sometimes she vomits. We've reached the end of our rope with her."

Sue's mother looks at me accusingly. I feel almost compelled to say, "Well, hell, it ain't my fault." With the guise of the clever psychologist I respond with the subtle, searching inquiry, "Any problems at home?"

She almost screams at me, "That's what I've been telling you. She's driving us crazy." I clarify, "No, I mean is there any other stress in your family?"

"What do you mean?" she asks suspiciously. "Well," my voice waivers uncertainly. I wonder now what I did mean. "Are there any major problems in your family other than Sue's difficulty?"

"Of course not," she replies defiantly. "My husband is making a great deal of money. We're building a new home; fifty-five thousand dollars," she adds in a modest undertone. "John and I have a fine home life. Oh, we have our little spats like most couples. But we always work them out. We love Sue dearly. But we just don't understand what is the matter. I know she's happy at home. It must be the school. I just know she must have a learning disability, and the school is just not helping her."

Sue and I talk. "I know what you're going to do," she says. "What?" I ask.

"Well, you're going to give me some tests to see what's wrong with me. Aren't you?" she adds.

"Do you think there's something wrong with you, Sue?" "No," she answers. "But mother does." She seems pleased with this observation.

I do all the things I know to do. We go through an intelligence test, a perceptual-motor scale, a projective test, and an interview. As a last resort we look for learning disabilities or suggestions of hyperactivity and impulsiveness.

I can find no evidence of learning difficulties. She is reading and spelling well above expected grade level. She has an IQ of 115 with no evidence of cognitive difficulties. Her perceptual-motor skills are better than expected for her chronological age. There is no suggestion of hyperactivity or distractability. But she is an uptight little girl. She clings to me dependently. She is always afraid her answers might be wrong, and she's excessively concerned about "how many I got right." She requires explicit parameters of response limits and tries to elaborate on any idea that I respond to with silence. Her observations of pictures are marked by the themes of trouble and struggle and loss of support. She draws a picture of her family that occupies only about one-fourth of the available space. The figures are clustered tightly together, staring out at the viewer in a rigid stance. Her fingernails are bitten to the quick, and she is fidgety and restless. "Where is mother now?" she asks several times. "In the waiting room," I reassure her.

I see a fearful, excessively dependent child who is much in need of security and support. "No," I tell her mother, "I don't find any evidence of a learning disability." I review my findings with her. Tentatively I express the feeling, "Is it possible that there is some stress at home that is contributing to this?"

"I don't see how," replies Sue's mother, "I told you we have a good life and a happy, successful one."

We set a time for an additional appointment to explore the matter further. But at the time of the next visit they fail to return. After a few days I call but get no answer. For awhile I wonder what has happened and think about Sue a bit. Gradually I forget Sue and her mother.

Weeks go by, and then I have a call from Sue's mother. "I want to schedule an appointment with you."

"Well, all right. But tell me, where have you been?"

She's silent a moment. "We've been living in a motel since John beat me up again and threw us out of the house."

"Why the hell didn't you tell me about that? I asked you if you had any problem, and you denied it." I'm incredulous.

She replies indignantly, "Sue had the problem, not us. We never let her see us fight, and she didn't know we had problems or arguments."

I sigh, having learned another lesson about sharing, which must go both ways. I just hope I can teach Sue's mother something about it too. "Sure, come on in. I'll see you next week."

Millie and her Kuder

I can't vouch for the validity of this story that I have heard about a young lady who was completing her training as a psychologist. But it rings true.

Mildred was beginning her internship in clinical practice, having finished her course work and her supervised therapy in role playing sessions with her fellow students. She was scheduled to see her first client that fateful afternoon. His problems revolved around an appropriate vocational choice and consequent needs to make proper educational plans.

Every client who comes to a counseling center with the stated problem of vocational choice (often they turn out to have every problem in the book except job planning difficulties) is assigned to take a battery of psychological tests under the supervision of a psychometrist. One of the more popular tests given to such clients is the Kuder Preference Record, a measure of vocational and job task interests and values. In the trade we call it simply "the Kuder."

Millie's initial interview with her client was scheduled for Office 1-C. This office had a one-way vision mirror, and adjoined an observation room equipped with several chairs where supervisors and clinical students could watch and listen to the struggling psychologist's feeble efforts. Incidentally, knowing you are being watched is a staggering load to carry when you are already in a panic. The room was wired for sound, and one could hear and see perfectly and clearly.

Curiously, the psychologist, who is always informed if he is to be observed, is much more traumatized by this procedure than the client seems to be. Usually when you tell the client that observers will be watching the session, he expresses mild interest and concern but quickly seems to forget after the session gets underway.

Anyhow, Millie was acutely aware that first day that she had an audience. She sits behind her desk nervously, thumbing through papers, checking the time and anxiously picking at her collar. Finally the client knocks, and Millie opens the door. She smiles warmly and looks pretty calm to her observers.

"Have a seat," she invites the young man with a wave of her hand.

Smilingly and with a suggestion of subtle intimacy, she pulls her chair from behind the desk and places it close to his.

The young man sits in his chair, clutching the sheaf of papers and summaries of test results that he brought with him from the psychometric testing session.

"I understand that you need some help in job and educational planning," says Millie.

"Yes," the client smiles anxiously.

Confidently Millie replies, "Fine, but first let me see your Kuder."

He stares in frozen shock, not a muscle moving. Millie stares back, eyeball to eyeball. She knows something is horribly wrong, but her mind can't tell her what it is. The scene fades as two stunned people are locked in a hypnotic rigidity.

"How did it end?" I ask the hysterical colleague who is telling me the story.

"I don't know," he gasps. "We all fell out of our chairs laughing, and the supervisor mercifully pulled the viewing curtain over the one-way mirror.

If it's not true as he tells it, it should be. All of us have made bigger fools of ourselves than that.

What is left of what you learn

Finally, after repeated episodes of embarrassment, failure, and stumbling ineptitude, you drop the techniques you've learned. You abandon the bedside manner, and you give up the business of conning and bluffing the people you are trying to help. You surrender the need to be powerful, to dominate, to direct someone else's life and how he should live it. You don't care what the client really thinks of you—at least that's no longer your primary concern. Finally, your major interest is in seeing that somebody who was hurting is feeling better; in seeing a constricted, fearful personality emerge into a free and trusting spirit. Your concern and interests shift from yourself to the one you would help. Being with him in a helpful way comes to be vastly more important than being right.

You grow in your ability to appreciate the seeker of help as an individual with unique, interesting, and powerful needs, wants, and feelings. You can see fear, feel it yourself; know his joy, share it with him. He isn't like anyone else in the world; and the more you can come to know him, the clearer you can see that he is living as bravely and as fully as he can in a world that is forbidding and hostile. Now I can sense his need to be known for what he is, whatever that may be. He tells me loudly, clearly, compellingly, "Look at me, I'm somebody. I am important, and I feel. I sorrow. I despair. I want security, love, appreciation, and attention, and when I can't get it, I'm frantic and afraid."

The only way I can be of help is to share myself in helpful ways. Honesty and careful sharing are the only "techniques" of value to me now. If these don't help, then I can't help. I have to learn that he doesn't have to believe as I do to be a valued person; he needn't live as I do to be real. He will not have to be someone other than himself to be free. The badly maligned Freud himself said, "A man should not strive to eliminate his complexes, but to get in accord with them; they are legitimately what directs his conduct in the world."

If I can teach him in his association and interaction with me that it is all right for him to be what he is and that I won't hurt him, and consequently the world won't hurt him, then he can begin to practice his uniqueness and his freedom, and that will extend mine too.

My favorite six-year-old once said, "I am not like any other person in the whole world." I'm not either. Neither are you.